WELFARE POLITICS IN BOSTON, 1910–1940

A VOLUME IN THE SERIES

Political Development of the American Nation:
Studies in Politics and History

Edited by JEROME M. MILEUR AND SIDNEY M. MILKIS

WELFARE POLITICS IN BOSTON, 1910–1940

SUSAN TRAVERSO

University of Massachusetts Press

Amherst and Boston

LC 2002015447
ISBN 1–55849–378–6

Designed by Dennis Anderson
Set in Minion with Optima display by Graphic Composition, Inc.
Printed and bound by The Maple-Vail Book Manufacturing Group

Library of Congress Cataloging-in-Publication Data

Traverso, Susan, 1959–
    Welfare politics in Boston, 1910–1940 / Susan Traverso.
        p. cm.—(Political development of the American nation)
    Includes bibliographical references and index.
    ISBN 1-55849-378-6 (acid free)
    1. Public welfare—Massachusetts—Boston—History. 2. Public welfare.
    3. Boston (Mass.)—Social conditions. I. Title. II. Series.

HV99.B6 T738 2003
361.6′1′0974461—dc21

                                                    2002015447

British Library Cataloguing-in-Publication Data are available.

For my parents and grandparents

CONTENTS

PREFACE

A STUDY OF welfare policy in Boston, this book explores the influence of political institutions and social relations on welfare policy, and the interplay between politics and social relations. Moreover, the local focus of this book highlights two influences on welfare policy often overlooked, ethnicity and religion. At the turn of the twentieth century, the influx of millions of foreign immigrants to American urban centers transformed social and political relations and, thus, the context for policy formation. The social and political incorporation of foreign immigrants shaped welfare policy as much as did the efforts by Progressive reformers to enlarge welfare programs. The establishment of Catholicism and Judaism as influential American religions had a bearing on ideas about individualism and collectivity and, thus, the philosophical underpinnings of policy formation. Interwoven with these ideological shifts were ideas about gender roles, the rights of men and women, and the distribution of resources to individuals and to individuals within families. Putting aside the tendency to use gender merely as a means of dividing policy initiatives or social reformers, this book examines gender within a specific social and political context, one redefined ethnically and religiously. Viewing political structures, social relations, and ideas together, this book uncovers the ways ethnic groups used conceptions of family-based citizenship to enlarge welfare provisions.

Public policy history has intellectual assets but also particular challenges. It can teach us the importance of the social and political contexts in which policy is crafted, the influence of individuals and groups of people on policy, and the impact of policy on the larger society. Policy studies can help us understand the political and economic structures, formal and informal, and the meaning of citizenship within those structures. We can explore the characteristics and identities we use to group people—race, gender, religion, ethnicity, economic status—and the ways groups have been entitled to and excluded from governmental programs and benefits. We can also measure the extent to which programs and benefits have defined the entitled and the marginalized. Finally, histories of public policy can uncover the ideological foundations of policy initiative and programs.

A significant challenge for histories of social welfare, however, is incorporating people, particularly the poor, in the analysis. Welfare case records can provide information about their lives, ideas, reaction to policy, and their ability to influence policy. But even those records are mediated through the voice of the social workers required to keep them. Social welfare historians have, nevertheless, endeavored to document the experience of the less advantaged members of our economic and political systems and the effort by the poor to ameliorate the suffering and lack of resources. But scholars— and readers—of public policy need always to recognize the limits of policy history to convey the experience of poor people.

A second tension between social welfare history and the lives of poor people is the uncertain relationship between studies of policy in the past and current policy initiatives. Public policy historians have been criticized for not protesting more vigorously the abolition in 1996 of Aid to Families with Dependent Children (AFDC), the federal program that guaranteed support to needy families. The failings of the system, however, was the very point of the advocates of welfare reform, even if many of them often put more blame on the poor for the system's failure than on society as a whole. The social welfare scholarship, like advocates of welfare reform, highlighted the limits of the American welfare system, particularly the aiding of children in poor families. Ample evidence illustrated that AFDC, though an entitlement program originating as part of the Social Security Act of 1935, had in practice and perception none of the guarantees or rights associated with the other social welfare programs established during the New Deal and enlarged over the next two decades, especially programs for unemployment, old age, and survivors insurance. The evidence also revealed that the history of public aid for families with dependent children told a story of mixed messages about combining mothering and paid labor force participation not to mention a tale of intrusiveness and control by social workers (many of them women) of poor families (disproportionately headed by women). Most scholars of social welfare could not honestly celebrate AFDC even if they believed that the government should provide aid to poor women with children.[1]

Like society as a whole and the policymakers who preceded them, scholars seem divided on whether welfare support should allow poor single mothers, like other women with husbands or families to support them, to focus on mothering exclusively and, in doing so, to be dependent. The Personal Responsibility and Work Opportunity Act in 1996 favored work over dependency, abolishing AFDC as a federal entitlement program, setting time limits on welfare support, and requiring states to institute workforce engagement for welfare recipients as much as possible.

The drop in welfare cases since 1996 indicates to some that welfare reform has worked; others want to ask the hard questions of welfare reform that social policy historians ask of the past practices. Who is benefiting from welfare reform and who isn't? Who is defining "benefiting"? Is welfare reform helping to diminish sexual and racial inequality or is it perpetuating legacies of discrimination based on gender and race? Do the divergent expectations of mothers regarding wage work and child care, based largely on class and marital status but also on race, contradict notions of equality of social citizenship, or will they evaporate as the combining of work and mothering again becomes the norm for nearly all women as it had been before the twentieth century? Finally, how do we as a society confront and cope with dependency in a culture that stresses independence and freedom of opportunity?[2]

Policy historians can raise such questions in contemporary policy debates. Even if answers to these questions vary, the questions make clear that welfare politics and policy are about much more than who gets a check in the mail. Welfare, meaning not only the care of the poor but also governmental support of all members of society, is both a response to unequal social and economic relations and a tool for crafting those relations. Ideas as much as political structure underlay welfare policy and those ideological underpinnings are often conflicted and even contradictory in a pluralistic society. The risk, then, is that the complexity introduced by these observations prevents historians and sociologists from engaging in contemporary debates over welfare policy. Complexity, however, is an antidote for the mythical notions of American ideals that undermine discussions about welfare. Contemporary debate about welfare reform, faith-based charities, and individual responsibility, like the earlier policy discussions, are constrained by American political and economic institutions, but they are also fueled by ideas that demand honest examination and debate in a truly democratic arena. That might be too much to hope for in a period of limited political engagement and of ideas stalemated by liberal and conservative dichotomies, but American history is marked by periods of debate about welfare that, while not always fully democratic were, nevertheless, times when we asked who was responsible for whom and why. Boston's struggle over welfare politics in the early twentieth century was just such a time.

I HAVE ENJOYED the support of numerous people and institutions while writing this book. Foremost, I am indebted to the Women's History program at the University of Wisconsin-Madison. Gerda Lerner, Linda Gordon, and Jeanne Boydston created a community of scholars that was both supportive and challenging. I am particularly thankful for Linda Gordon's guidance, criticism, and encouragement on this project. Her own research on social welfare history set a high standard of excellence. Thomas Archdeacon and John Cooper helped put my work into the larger frame of political and immigration history, and Ann Orloff provided a sociological perspective. My colleagues in the history department at North Central College have supported and encouraged my work on this book, and the exchange of ideas with colleagues from other disciplines at the college has enriched my thinking and perspective on history.

Financial assistance from a variety of sources supported this project. At Wisconsin, fellowships from the History Department, a Marie Christine Kohler Residential Fellowship, and the Gerda Lerner Fellowship in Women's History; in addition, a Woodrow Wilson Grant in Women's Studies supported early research. North Central College provided summer writing grants and a leave from teaching to complete the manuscript.

Archivists at Simmons College, the Catholic Archdiocese of Boston, the American Jewish Historical Society, the University of Massachusetts Boston, the Boston Public Library, the Massachusetts Archives, the Massachusetts Historical Society, and Schlesinger Library as well as librarians at the State Library of Massachusetts, the Boston Athenaeum, the University of Wisconsin, and North Central College provided important guidance and support for my research. The readers and the editors at the University of Massachusetts Press helped sharpen my argument and writing, and James Connolly's close review of the manuscript provided valuable insight on the political setting of early twentieth-century Boston.

When all is said and done, though, it is my family—the Traversos and the Taylors—whom I must thank the most. My father's and now my sister's work with poor families reminds me that the well-being of people is what really is at stake in the unfolding of social welfare policy. The environmental planning work of my husband, Kent Taylor, also links policy with societal good. Kent has endured long discussions about welfare history, welfare reform, and social policy, and I thank him. His friendship and love are my steadiest source of support.

ABBREVIATIONS

AC   Associated Charities

ADC   Aid to Dependent Children

AJHS   American Jewish Historical Society

AFDC   Aid to Families with Dependent Children

BPA   Boston Provident Association

CCB   Catholic Charitable Bureau

CSA   Council of Social Agencies

DPW   Department of Public Welfare

FinCom   Finance Commission

FJC   Federated Jewish Charities

FWA   Family Welfare Association, Federated Jewish Charities

FWS   Family Welfare Society

OAA   Old Age Assistance

OP   Overseers of the Poor

OPW   Overseers of the Public Welfare

PCCB   *Proceedings of the City Council of Boston*

PCJP   Papers of the Combined Jewish Philanthropies

UHBA   United Hebrew Benevolent Association

WPA   Works Progress Administration

WELFARE POLITICS IN BOSTON, 1910–1940

INTRODUCTION:

PLACING WELFARE HISTORY IN BOSTON

I
N THIS BOOK I trace Boston's social welfare history in its own terms. In doing so, I resist the more common approach, namely, the measuring of welfare policy against abstract notions of statecraft, whether conservative or liberal. Between 1910 and 1940, Boston's charity system was transformed into a public assistance program as the responsibility for poor relief shifted from the city's Protestant, Catholic, and Jewish private charities to the public welfare department. The result was a broader, though still fragmented, safety net for the city's poor and a reconfiguration of public and private responsibility. As the dates indicate, the move toward enlarged public relief in Boston began not with the introduction of New Deal initiatives during the 1930s but, instead, over the twenty years preceding the passage of federal welfare legislation. During those decades, local political and social conflict reshaped the city's welfare policies and programs. The "welfare politics" that emerged during this period are the focus of this book.

My contention that the social welfare system that emerged in Boston between 1910 and 1940 was fragmented and inadequate supports interpretations of American social policy which highlight the limited public commitment to aid for the poor. However, rather than suggesting that this outcome represented a falling short of some ideal welfare state model, I argue that Boston's incomplete welfare system was the product of the social conflict, cultural dissimilarities, and antagonistic politics which characterized that urban center in the first half of the twentieth century. The politics surrounding public welfare grew out of the social and political changes taking place in Boston as the city's immigrant-stock population became a majority and as ethnic politicians, predominately Irish, gained control of city government. Played out in the formal political arena and among the city's private charities, the welfare politics of this period challenged the Protestant leaders and Yankee politicians whose long family ties to the city provided them social, economic, and political advantage. The political struggle over welfare

1

eventually weakened the control that white Protestant groups had over Boston's public and private poor relief programs and created opportunities for immigrant politicians and Catholic and Jewish charities to influence welfare policy. More than a tale of declension and ascension, however, the history of welfare in early twentieth-century Boston is a story of political and cultural compromise between competing groups.

Conflicting ideas about the purpose of charity and the role of the state were at the heart of Boston's welfare politics. Yankee politicians and spokesmen of the city's Protestant-led sectarian charities considered poor relief a necessary social function but believed that it should be distributed only as a last resort. They maintained that the scope of relief operations should be limited and that reliance on charity should be discouraged. To this end, they supported a small public relief program, the Overseers of the Poor, but insisted that charity remain primarily a function of private organizations and families. In contrast, the leaders of Boston's Catholic and Jewish charities as well as the emerging non-Yankee political leadership were more willing to recognize the need for poor relief and less apt to regard the acceptance of charity as either a societal or individual weakness. Their view on poor relief led them to advocate enlarged relief efforts both public and private.

Even as ethnic and religious conflicts fueled disagreements about welfare, so too did concepts about gender roles. The welfare programs created in the early twentieth century were all deeply gendered. By this, I do not only mean that some programs benefited women while others benefited men or that certain programs enjoyed the support of men while others gained support from women—although both situations were true. Welfare programs were gendered in that both their mission and their administration reflected a mixture of perceptions and realities about men and women. These ideas about the role of women and men promoted the passage and funding of some welfare programs while leading to the defeat or limited funding of others.

Between 1910 and 1940, gendered arguments determined relief priorities. The campaign for widows' pensions in the early 1910s won broad popular support even as public welfare programs that would primarily benefit men, such as unemployment insurance and old age pensions, did not. Women were understood to be, and usually were, dependent, whereas men were envisioned as independent wage earners for whom welfare dependency was considered unmanly. Mothers' Aid became a catalyst for public welfare expansion and overpowered constraints on public assistance. More generous

grant sizes and the introduction of case work methodology—both consequences of this program's maternal focus—increased the amount spent by
the city on poor relief and the size of the public welfare staff. Moreover, this
welfare program for poor women required the public welfare department to
hire women caseworkers for the first time in its history.

The public welfare program and the political debate over welfare changed
focus, however, in the 1920s, as prolonged periods of unemployment led
ethnic politicians to demand greater attention to the needs of unemployed
men, particularly those with families to support. This increased focus on
the needs of male breadwinners recast public aid as an acceptable source of
income for unemployed men. Using the rhetoric of the Mothers' Aid campaign, politicians enlarged the idea of "acceptable dependency" to include
men who depended on employment to provide for their own dependents
and who needed assistance during times of joblessness to fulfill the role of
family breadwinner. As part of this campaign, reliance on public aid was dis-
sociated from "unmanliness." If anything, the campaign reinforced a man's
duties as head of a household as much as Mothers' Aid recognized women's
responsibilities for their children. This gendered argument not only lessened
the stigma of male dependency on public welfare; it also encouraged unprecedented use of public aid by unemployed men during the 1920s. In fact,
political support for the unemployed and funding of public aid for unemployment relief overshadowed the Mothers' Aid program, the very program
used to justify welfare expansion. As aid to unemployed men increased, the
funding for Mothers' Aid decreased. Moreover, advocates of expanded unemployment aid criticized the close supervision of Mothers' Aid recipients,
a social work methodology that the critics did not want expanded to general
relief cases.

The creation and implementation of Boston's gendered welfare programs
was further complicated by the divergent ideas about gender and social
policy held by the city's private charity leaders. The Protestant charity leaders, along with Boston's Yankee establishment, held an individualistic view
of social relations. According to this view, the market economy provided
opportunities for financial independence for men and, perhaps, even for
women. More than Catholic and Jewish participants in the welfare debate,
Protestant charity leaders and politicians identified women as potentially
independent economic actors. In general, these leaders and politicians were
not opposed to women working outside the home, and they believed that
poor women, even mothers, might be able to support themselves and their

families. By the same token, they believed that poor women were personally and morally responsible as individuals for their plight—an attitude that supported belief in limited and highly supervised poor relief programs.

The Catholic and Jewish charity leaders, along with their counterparts in the political arena, did not share the Protestants' individualistic interpretation of social relations or their faith in the market system. Seeing capitalism more as a system of dependency than independence, they did not see self-sufficiency as either possible or necessary. Their conception of family relations mirrored their larger worldview. Dependency of women and children, they believed, was inevitable and desirable. In general, the Catholic charity leaders and Irish politicians who crafted welfare policy at this time condemned mothers for working outside the home. Jewish leaders were less critical of the economic activities of women but, nevertheless, considered employment by mothers outside the home undesirable and an indication of a failure of the social and economic system. To most Catholic and Jewish leaders, dependency on social welfare programs was not necessarily or morally detrimental. On the contrary, they believed that public assistance to the needy was both necessary and moral.

However, even as Protestant, Catholic, and Jewish charity and political leaders expressed different ideas about social relations, they shared a vision of gender relations based on an idealized family headed by a male breadwinner with a dependent wife and children. In this idealized picture of the family, which described few poor families, dependency within families was assumed while the family's need and/or right to be dependent on public aid became the political issue. Ignoring the differences among families, particularly between male-headed and female-headed households, Boston's leaders struggled to determine welfare policy for idealized families.

Shared ideas about the family enabled Boston's leaders to compromise on welfare policy, especially during the Depression. During the crisis of the 1930s, politicians and private charity leaders crafted welfare policy primarily in response to the needs of unemployed families, defined as the idealized model of a male breadwinner with a dependent wife and children. Relief to unemployed men dwarfed the support provided to "traditional" public relief recipients, typically women with dependent children, the elderly poor, and the sick. Even more than during the 1920s, the public welfare department took on a masculine orientation. The focus on the unemployed led the public welfare office to enlarge its staff of male visitors, primarily patronage hires with little experience or training in either charity or social work. The national commitment to public relief, embodied in New Deal legislation, furthered this local trend since it, too, was primarily a response to the crisis of male unemployment and the inability of localities to support families of unemployed men. Even the federal categorical aid programs, Old Age Assistance and Aid to Dependent Children, that were introduced with the Social Security Act in 1935 gained support because of the unemployment crisis, though the demands for those programs predated the Depression. The result, locally, was a tremendously enlarged public welfare system justified, for the most part, by the scope of the Depression and by the local political support for aid to unemployed men.

Increasingly described by politicians—Republicans and Democrats alike—as a "legitimate" and "unstigmatized" source of financial aid, large-scale public assistance to the needy, including the unemployed, had become a permanent public function by the late 1930s. But constructed as it was out of political compromise and gendered ideals, rather than realities, the foundation of Boston's welfare system was hardly secure. When the war economy began to take men off the relief rolls, local political support for welfare weakened. Public aid recipients became suspect once again, and welfare reforms intending to cut the level of spending on public aid gained momentum. Divisions among welfare programs sharpened as categorical relief programs competed for funding when the welfare budget faced its first fiscal constraints in over a decade. Differentiation among public aid programs, intensified by federal policy and funding differences, produced a public welfare system in Boston that, although enlarged, remained fragmented and inadequate. Moreover, the system became once again of little local political consequence.

The early twentieth-century political struggle over public welfare highlighted the differences between private charities. The city's Protestant, Catholic, and Jewish charities had varying levels of influence on public policy, and their access to the state changed as the social and political climate shifted. Both during the campaign for widows' pensions in the 1910s and during public welfare expansion in the following decade, Catholic and Jewish charities expressed support for the enlarged public welfare expenditures and for the increasing tendency by the city's poor to turn to the Overseers for assistance. The Protestant charity leaders, in contrast, strongly opposed the increased spending on public relief that the passage of Mothers' Aid sparked and that continued during the 1920s. Part of the explanation for the different reactions lay in these charities' different philosophical views on poverty and dependence, but economic and political considerations also contributed to the stances of these private charities. Protestant charity leaders feared the increased taxes associated with enlarged welfare spending and the loss of their informal control over the city's charity system as much as "moral" consequences of dependence by the poor on public funds. Catholic and Jewish charity leaders, conversely, saw enlarged welfare operations as potentially benefiting their organizations. New public welfare spending might lighten these private charities' relief burdens and open new means for Catholic and Jewish charities to influence public welfare policy.

Ideologically and politically at odds, Boston's Protestant, Catholic, and Jewish charities did not offer unified support for an enlarged public welfare system. Between 1910 and 1935, these organizations relinquished nearly all of their relief functions to the city's public welfare department, but the history of that "surrender" was hardly uniform. Jewish charity leaders were the most convinced of the potential benefit of a liberal state policy toward public relief; as a result, they pressed for increased public responsibility and directed their clients toward public welfare programs whenever possible. Associating the state with Protestant control, Boston's Catholic charitable leaders were suspicious of enlarged public welfare programs at the beginning of the century. Once assured of the growing Catholic influence in city and state politics, however, Boston's Catholic charities joined the Jewish leaders in pressing for public welfare enlargement and encouraged their clients to make use of public welfare programs. Resentful that the political success of Catholics had moved public welfare policy beyond their control, Protestant charity leaders remained firmly opposed to the increased use of public relief programs and to greater funding for public aid. Only in the depth of the Depression and with the prospect that the New Deal administration might limit the local political control over public welfare did the city's Protestant charity leaders begin to concede the need for a large-scale public welfare program.

As public welfare enlarged, Boston's private charities relinquished their poor relief functions and retreated from the politics of public welfare. Defining themselves as professional providers of social services rather than as sources of financial assistance, these private charities saw their social and political importance weaken. The bifurcation of public and private assistance diminished the differences among these private organizations. The most significant result of the private charities' withdrawal from public welfare policy, however, was the construction, real and perceived, of the public welfare department as less service-oriented and less professional. Thus, although public welfare replaced private charity as the primary source of financial assistance to the poor, it retained the stigma that had long characterized poor relief. Shaped (or perhaps misshaped) by politics, welfare became a necessary but hardly celebrated government function.

SINCE THE early 1990s a rich scholarship on social welfare history has emerged. Most influential has been the literature urging a "state-centered" approach to policy analysis that demands an examination of political institutions to explain the development (or lack of development) of programs of social provisions. Setting aside theories that cite modernization, urbanization, or advanced capitalism as precipitating state-run welfare programs as well as the claim that an American ethos of individualism explains the limited development of public welfare programs in the United States, these scholars look to the political institutions out of which the welfare programs grew to understand their origins and development. Boston's welfare history confirms many finding of these political histories of social policy, including their core argument that the decentralized American state structure along with universal suffrage for men impeded the growth of a centralized welfare state similar to those in other advanced industrial nations.[1]

By studying welfare policies at the level of the municipality, however, this book examines aspects of social policy development that scholars of welfare state formation have not fully addressed, namely the impact of the ethnic and religious conflicts of early twentieth-century America. The influx of new immigrant groups as well as the ascendancy of immigrant-stock politicians in city government sparked heated debate and conflict about the role of the state and the relationship of these new groups to the state. While urban and immigration historians have stressed the impact of different ethnic and religious groups in American society, historians of social welfare have underestimated the significance of social changes in the early twentieth century, especially in large urban areas, to the formation of welfare policy. What focus scholars have had on ethnicity and religion has largely concerned the relationship between native-born social workers and immigrant clients, a relationship often troubled by culture dissimilarities. The cultural conflicts of the early twentieth century, expressed primarily through religious identity, shaped welfare policy as much as they did relationships between social workers and clients, especially as Catholics and Jews gained influence in policy creation.[2]

The local focus of this book also allows for a more integrated analysis of gender and social policy. Gender analyses of welfare programs have suffered from too narrow a focus on particular welfare programs, often those for women, or too abstract a comparison between welfare programs divided along gender lines. Both of these approaches tend to divorce welfare policy development from broader social and political trends and from other welfare programs. By looking at a range of welfare initiatives within a specific context, I emphasize that the gender constructions embedded within welfare programs worked within changing social and political contexts. Moreover, I show the interrelationship between welfare programs for women and men. Although this book illuminates the important differences between programs for women and men and their significance to the development of a modern welfare system, it rejects theories that see U.S. policy development as one bifurcated between male and female "welfare streams" or by "maternal" and "paternal" visions of welfare. Instead of imposing essentialist categories onto the history of welfare, I examine welfare programs in the specific social and political context from which they developed, paying close attention to the significant religious, ethnic, and class differences among men and women in the first part of the twentieth century. Framed this way, gender is understood not as what divided social policy but as what assured it political consensus across religious, ethnic, and class divisions.[3]

B OSTON PROVIDES a rich context in which to examine the impact of politics and ethnicity on the development of social welfare policy. In 1910, 74 percent of Boston's residents were immigrants or children of immigrants: it is safe to say that immigration had transformed the city. Protestant Bostonians, many with colonial roots, had dominated the city before the influx of a large number of impoverished foreign immigrants. Starting in the 1820s and 1830s, the arrival of large numbers of Irish immigrants altered what had been a relatively homogeneous city population and sparked ethnic conflict. The arrival of "new immigrants," mainly Italians and Russian Jews, after the 1880s only intensified ethnic tension in Boston. For many of the city's white native-born men and women, the growing immigrant population represented a threat to Boston's political and cultural institutions and a potential drain on public services, paid for primarily through local tax revenues. Hoping to slow immigration, influential Bostonians spearheaded the national movement for immigration restriction, furthering ethnic tensions within the city.[4]

Differences in economic opportunity further divided Boston's native-born and immigrant populations. As the twentieth century opened, native-born white Bostonians enjoyed greater economic security and opportunity while the immigrant stock, along with the city's small black population, had comparatively few social and economic advantages. Most of Boston's immigrants arrived poor and uneducated, and they saw little social mobility during their lifetimes. Nearly half of all male immigrants held menial unskilled or semiskilled laboring jobs while just slightly more than a tenth of native-born workers held similar low-paying positions. Opportunities for children of immigrants remained inferior to those of the native-born white population. Not until the second generation did social and economic opportunities offer some white ethnics the possibility of a middle-class life.[5]

During the early twentieth century, local politics accentuated social and economic divisions within the city, largely setting the city's poorer immigrant stock against its wealthier native-born residents. During the late nineteenth century, politics of accommodation had opened some political doors to the city's immigrant populations while reserving most political power for the native-born, mainly Yankee Republicans. The sheer number of foreign-stock residents along with the success of Irish politicians at the ward level, however, engendered a more antagonistic political climate by the beginning of the twentieth century. During this time some Irish Catholics improved their economic lot and made inroads to political control of the city. Boston's black population, residentially segregated and comparatively small in number, was overshadowed in this political context.[6]

Party alignment in twentieth-century Boston contributed to the polarization of the political climate and further divided immigrant and native-born Bostonians. In general, party membership in twentieth-century Boston was a function of ethnic and socioeconomic identity. The introduction of women voters in 1920 only strengthened this correlation. Old-stock citizens dominated the Republican Party while the Irish swelled the Democratic Party, though hardly as a unified force. The new immigrants were pushed and pulled between the parties but eventually aligned with the Democrats. Irish ward bosses were careful to accommodate the newer immigrants moving into formerly Irish neighborhoods, and the ward bosses shared a minimum of rewards with their new constituents to gain their vote. Italians rapidly sided with the Democratic Party both locally and nationally. The Jewish vote was not as easily won and was divided along class lines during the first two decades of the twentieth century, with wealthier Jews voting Republican and poorer Jews more open to Democratic candidates at the local level. The alignment of Jews with the Republican Party, however, shifted during the twenties as did black support. With the New Deal, Jews of all classes as well as the city's black voters aligned with the Democratic Party. Even as Democrats gained control of city politics, however, no "boss" ever wielded control of the party, not even the city's infamous mayor, James Michael Curley. Moreover, class differences among the city's ethnic populations, always present, became more pronounced, particularly among the Irish, in the 1930s. But even without a unified Democratic force and with a more accommodating Irish middle class emerging during the Depression, the political allegiances in early twentieth-century Boston were largely dichotomized as immigrant-stock politicians, a growing number of them Democrat, vied against Yankee Republicans. In this contentious social and political setting, the conflicts surrounding public welfare provisions took on a particular intensity.[7]

Boston's residents, immigrant and native-born alike, had long recognized the need for a social response to the needs of the poor. Boston hosted a plethora of private social welfare organizations as well as a public aid program administered by the city's Overseers of the Poor. In 1910, over 2,000 private charitable agencies operated in the city, and leaders of these organizations participated in national charity organizations. Seeing Boston as a model for the nation and often bragging that it led the nation in charitable enterprises and concern for the poor, the leaders of Boston's Catholic, Jewish, and white Protestant charities were engaged in the development of modern welfare policy. The absence of the city's black leaders from this discussion, however, should not be misunderstood as a lack of concern or activism. Like the city's foreign immigrants, black Bostonians were disproportionably poor but, unlike the growing ranks of white ethnics, blacks represented just over 2 percent of the city's population. Patterns of segregation persisted in the arena of social services, and most poor blacks relied on white-founded institutions that served only blacks or, more commonly, on black organizations and churches. In both instances, the ethos of "self-help" predominated. The result was that, as an observer in 1914 noted, few "Negroes fall into the hands of public and private charity." Even more significant, however, was that black charity leaders were not part of the political debate that shaped public welfare. The politics of welfare in Boston was a politics of whiteness, which was not the only aspect of its failing but one which bears serious consideration in our understanding of social welfare history in this country.[8]

This book does not argue that Boston was typical of other urban centers in the early twentieth century, however, or that its welfare history matched the policies in other cities. Changes in other urban centers did not mirror the changes in Boston, a city more Irish-Catholic than any other American city and with less ethnic diversity than industrial cities like Chicago and Pittsburgh. In fact, Boston had a much smaller black population than nearly every other large city at the time. Nevertheless, Boston, like urban centers across the nation, was a site of large-scale immigration and cultural conflict. By 1930, it was only one of seventeen cities where at least 50 percent of the population was immigrant stock. In general, foreign immigration produced an exodus of native-born residents from the nation's cities, leaving open the possibility for an increased level of influence by ethnic politicians at the municipal level. In these cities, as in Boston, heated debates over public welfare ensued as the social and political composition underwent change, the result being stronger support for enlarged governmental support for public welfare.[9]

Boston's welfare politics suggest more than the enduring power of localism in determining welfare. The political and social conflicts from which this city's fragmented welfare program emerged did not retard welfare policy; in fact, they determined welfare policy. In this way, the local social and political conflicts of this period hold clues as to the origin and characteristics of the American welfare system itself. While this single case study cannot explain the whole, the history of Boston's struggle over welfare suggests that the social, religious, and political conflict in early twentieth-century urban America is crucial to our understanding not only why the United States did not develop a welfare state comparable to those in other Western democracies but also what structures and values defined the system that did emerge. In Boston, ethnic and religious groups pressed for expanded public welfare provisions as much as, if not more than, native-born Progressive reformers did, and they met staunch opposition from the native-born Protestant leaders of the city. The enlarged and yet fragmented public welfare program that emerged represented a political and cultural compromise among the city's competing political and religious groups, based largely on a shared ideal of families headed by male breadwinners. We will better understand the origins of our fragmented welfare system if we trace its emergence in early twentieth-century urban centers, locations of competing interests and ideas and sites of political and cultural compromise. This study of Boston is an effort to do just that.

1 BOSTON'S CHARITY SYSTEM

A N EXTENSIVE and diverse charity system existed in Boston at the turn of the twentieth century. With a tradition of public responsibility and a burgeoning, largely poor, immigrant population, Boston supported over two hundred religious and nonsectarian private charities as well as a publicly funded relief program, the Overseers of the Poor. Dispensing what was called at the time "outdoor relief," these programs aided the poor in their homes and offered an alternative to institutional, or "indoor," relief. Organized around religious, ethnic, or occupational identity, these charities generally cared for their own. The Society of St. Vincent de Paul, for example, aided needy Catholics; the German Aid Society reserved its funds for ethnic Germans; and the Leather Trade Benevolent Society assisted families of its tradesmen. Since their funds were limited, their aid was usually a token gesture hardly sufficient to support a poor man, woman, or family, forcing the poor to piece together support from any number of these organizations. Nevertheless, the charity of Boston's public and private relief agencies spared some of the poor the trauma and embarrassment of going to the public poorhouse, institutions that divided families, housing the destitute in bleak dormitory arrangements. Outdoor relief, in contrast, provided widows with children a chance to keep their families together, gave the aged and infirm some assistance, and supplemented the wages of the working poor by aiding families during periods of economic downturn or illness. Offering small cash grants or aid in kind—food, coal, and clothing—Boston's charities provided needed assistance to the city's poor.[1]

In the nineteenth century, Boston's charity system depended on the cooperation of private and public charities. Declaring that "municipal relief and private charity should supplement each other and act in union," the city had constructed a Charity Building in 1869 on Hawkins Street in downtown Boston. It was to this building that the city's poor came seeking assistance.

The Charity Building housed the headquarters of the Overseers of the Poor as well as offices for several of the leading private charities, including the Associated Charities, the Boston Provident Association, the Federated Jewish Charities, and the Society of St. Vincent de Paul. The city owned the building and charged the private charities only the heating costs of their offices. The close proximity of the offices encouraged cooperation; the agencies housed in the Charity Building often referred applicants among themselves and sometimes shared the support of particular cases.[2]

Though headquartered in a public building, the city's charity system was dominated by private charities. Their combined giving outstripped the public Overseers' annual budget as did their caseloads. Moreover, both charity officials and the poor considered private aid better than public relief. Private charities tended to provide larger amounts of aid, and reliance on their aid did not carry the stigma of public dependency. In addition, private charities operated with greater flexibility than the Overseers of the Poor, who were tied to state guidelines regarding residency. As a result, the Overseers usually aided only the most destitute, and a smaller number of the city's poor, than the private charities.

Male leadership characterized the relief operations of Boston's public and private charities. Until the 1890s, only men served on the board of the Overseers of the Poor, and even after that, they remained the clear majority of members. All of the visiting staff of the Overseers was male as were the secretary and treasurer, who were responsible for the daily operations of the city's charity efforts. Men directed the leading private charities as well. Even the Associated Charities, which boasted of its female volunteer corps of friendly visitors, had male boards of directors and presidents during this time. Distributing relief—whether in kind or cash—distinguished these organizations from other benevolent and reform associations. The latter groups proved important opportunities for women's leadership, but Boston's relief agencies remained under the direction of men.[3]

During much of the nineteenth century, accommodation prevailed in the relations among the city's charities and in the broader social and political relations in the city. With the influx of new immigrant groups toward the end of the nineteenth century, however, the city's social and political relations became more antagonistic. In this atmosphere, the differences among the city's charities became more pronounced. Among the private charities, religious identity increasingly defined these differences, as the city's private relief programs began to consolidate into larger Protestant, Catholic, and Jew-

ish organizations. The intensified religious identities of the city's major relief agencies helped dilute some of the ethnic differences in Boston between
older German Jews and new Jewish immigrants from Russia and between
the city's Irish and Italian Catholics. At the same time, though, religious
divisions between private charities tended to accentuate the more general
ethnic division in Boston: white native-born Protestants against the growing immigrant and immigrant-stock population. Ironically, the movement
toward religiously defined relief organizations had begun when Boston's
more liberal Protestants proposed the creation of nonsectarian charities.
Both nostalgic for the relatively homogeneous society that Boston had been
until then and fearful about social change, a number of the city's liberal
Protestants saw nonsectarian charity as an answer to the plight of poor immigrants as well as a means of maintaining Protestant influence. However,
the charities they founded were nonsectarian only insofar as they served a
mixed population. Established and led by white native-born Protestants,
these organizations forwarded the beliefs of their leadership even if they
did not overtly proselytize. Equally as significant was that Boston's Catholics and Jews viewed these nonsectarian charities as Protestant, and, in response, supported efforts to consolidate and, thereby, to expand the power
of their own charitable organizations.[4]

Private Charities: Protestant, Catholic, and Jewish

The Boston Provident Association (BPA), founded in 1851, and the Associated Charities (AC), founded in 1879, were Boston's leading nonsectarian
charity organizations and were at the center of Protestant charitable en-
deavor. These charities not only claimed no denominational affiliation;
they also aided people regardless of their ethnic or religious identities. As
the influx of immigrants increased, the proportion of foreign-born among
their recipients grew, reaching 56 percent of the Associated Charities' cases
by 1917. Nevertheless, both the Provident and the Associated remained controlled and directed by native-born Protestants. Their boards included well
connected, financially secure members of Boston society, and their staffs represented leaders—male and female—in the emerging field of social work,
both locally and nationally. Russell G. Fessenden, president of the American Trust Company, was the chief officer of the Provident, and William H.
Pear, "dean of New England social work," oversaw the daily operations.
Charles P. Putnam, a respected physician, and later John F. Moors, of the

brokerage house Moors and Cabot, were the chief officers of the Associated Charities. Alice L. Higgins and Fred R. Johnson, both important leaders in the Massachusetts Conference of Social Work and in the National Conference of Charities and Corrections, supervised the offices of the Associated.[5]

The BPA and the AC reflected the practices of the "scientific charity" movement of the late nineteenth century. Both agencies relied on "visitors" to interview applicants in their homes, to determine their need on an individual basis, and to monitor the "moral and material progress" of their clients. The agencies shared information about relief applicants through a "confidential exchange," and they encouraged other social service agencies to use and to support the exchange. Casework practice as well as interagency cooperation, they believed, could cure poverty scientifically and, thus, assure the positive evolution of society. "The character of the future American is at stake in every one of these [poor] families," reported the Associated Charities in 1910.[6]

These Protestant organizations blamed poverty on individual and family failure. In their assessment of poor families, they seldom identified economics alone as the cause of hardship but usually coupled financial difficulties with problems they saw as related to immorality. "The mere lack of money usually forms but a small part of the total sum of the need," Pear, general agent of the BPA, said in 1911. Accordingly, he believed the aim was "building up family strength, resourcefulness, and independence." The Associated Charities made a similar observation: "From the consideration of these nearly wrecked families, we gather first, that the key to their unsuccess is character." These charity officials often considered being unable to provide economically and being morally "unfit" one and the same.[7]

Given their moral interpretation of poverty, Protestant charities made supervision and guidance of the poor an integral part of their programs. When giving food orders, for example, the Provident asked grocers to note the items purchased on the back of the orders so the visitors could later "see ways in which they can give advice about family supplies." Moreover, neither agency hid its condescending attitude toward the poor. "Visitors," according to the secretary of the Associated, had to "have the courage to take an apparently worthless family and give it every opportunity of self-betterment, working with a faith that will not be daunted even in the face of undeniable failure."[8]

Fearing that cash relief might be poorly spent, the BPA and the AC primarily limited their relief to aid in kind—food, coal, and clothing. They made cash disbursements, usually three or four dollars a week, only in cases they considered "permanent" because of illness, old age, or widowhood. At its founding in 1879, the AC had criticized any form of poor relief, claiming that it had the potential to pauperize the poor and to discourage self-sufficiency. To the founders of the Associated, moral support and guidance through "friendly visiting" were of more aid to the poor than relief. By the early twentieth century, however, the AC regularly referred poor families to both public and private sources of material relief, and even dispensed relief directly. Both organizations limited the amount of their aid to below the level of full support. Doing so, they believed, would discourage the poor from becoming dependent on relief.[9]

From their founding, both the Provident and the Associated cooperated with the Overseers of the Poor. Neither organization sought to replace the public department or to channel public funds through private charities. The movement against public welfare that took root in the 1880s and 1890s in Philadelphia, New York, and other cities did not find ground in Boston during the same period. Confidence in the work of the public Overseers of the Poor remained solid among the city's native-born charity leaders. The Board of Overseers was composed largely of men and women from the same backgrounds as the Protestant charity leaders, namely native-born white Protestants with ties either to the business community or to "sectarian" charity efforts. Like the leaders of the Provident and the Associated, the Overseers advocated a limited program of public poor relief. The Protestant charities exchanged information about applicants with the Overseers, and the organizations collaborated in determining which cases should be aided with public funds and which with private funds. The result was that few cases, usually the most poor and destitute, relied on public aid.[10]

The city's Protestant charity leaders were actively involved in national social work organizations. They supported the emergence of professional social work and advocated the new practices associated with it, including specialized training for staff, casework methodology, and the compiling of social statistics. However, they represented the conservative wing of this new field. Unlike many in the settlement movement, for instance, they did not see charity as a means of removing the barriers between the rich and the poor. They were also more conservative than the proponents of social insurance, who promoted an enlarged state role in welfare. Boston's Protestant charity leaders also criticized proposals for old age pensions, public health insurance, and widows' pensions.

Although conservative politically, the leaders of the Provident and the Associated were more open-minded about family structure than many of their contemporaries. Mute on the issue of women's suffrage—a divisive battle in Massachusetts—the leaders of these charities, particularly those of the more women-focused Associated Charities, nevertheless expressed ideas that reflected the emerging feminism of the early twentieth century. While they were harsh critics of human failings, they did not include divorce among those failings. Moreover, while they did not overtly advocate specific birth control practices, they criticized large families, associating them with a lack of sexual control. At the same time, however, the leaders of these charities expressed concern for the mothers of these large families, on whom the burden of many children fell the hardest, especially when a husband's death removed the principal source of support. These leaders looked less critically on women who worked outside the home than many of their contemporaries did; they were certainly less critical of wage-earning women than many middle-class social reformers of their times. Their views of women's wage work derived not only from their practical experience with poor families that often relied on several incomes to survive but also from their individualistic view of society. Their expectation that individuals could determine their moral and economic fate prompted them to see women as more than victims and permanent dependents.[11]

Boston's Protestant charity leaders often portrayed themselves as representing all private charities in Boston. They were anxious to work with Catholic and Jewish charities and eager to standardize and to regulate both public and private relief in the city. They met some success working with Jewish charity leaders, many of whom, like themselves, were engaged in national social work organizations, but cooperation with Catholic charities proved more difficult.

The Catholic Charitable Bureau (CCB) was the central source of Catholic relief during the early twentieth century. Founded by the Archdiocese in 1903, the Bureau aimed to unify the city's numerous Catholic charities that were operating at the parish and neighborhood level. The creation of the CCB was, in many ways, an attempt by the Archdiocese to assert its control over the charitable endeavors of both Boston's Catholic lay organizations, like the Society of St. Vincent de Paul, and the numerous orders of sisters.

However, the Bureau was also an effort by the Church to protect the city's growing Catholic population and to strengthen Catholic charity overall. Unlike the mission of the Provident and the Associated, the Bureau's mission was to defend the poor against Protestant charity efforts as much as it was to serve them. Its advocacy for the poor was part of the Church's broader effort to carve out a place for Catholics within the dominant Protestant culture of Boston.[12]

At its inception, the CCB took a defensive position toward both public welfare and the Protestant charities. Its first campaign was an effort to require the state to place Catholic children who were wards of the state in Catholic foster homes. The campaign was thwarted by the city and state boards of child welfare, both of which were dominated by white native-born Protestants who refused to supply information about Catholic children to the CCB. Even after the state passed legislation in 1905 assuring the placement of Catholic children in Catholic homes, however, the Bureau remained suspicious of state-directed welfare programs. Thus, when proposals for a state-funded widows' pension began circulating, the Bureau opposed them and set up its own relief program. Benefiting from the direct support of the Archdiocese, the bureau's relief operations quickly superseded the charity programs at the parish levels, becoming the major source of financial aid to needy Catholic families.[13]

Unlike the Protestant charities, the Bureau did not link poverty to individual failing but, instead, blamed environmental factors for the plight of the poor. The accusatory tone so prevalent in the reports of the Provident and the Associated was not used in the Bureau's reports. The Bureau's directors linked poverty to situations beyond the control of the poor, like widowhood or shifts in the labor market. They cited factors such as high rents and expensive coal as the source of the difficulties the poor faced, not moral or family failings. When asked to tabulate or to summarize the difficulties their recipients faced, the Bureau usually specified "economic" as the major concern.

The Bureau took a defensive and protective posture in all of its work. Unlike the Protestant charities, it seldom criticized the poor, and it rarely included specific information about recipients in its reports. It often refused to participate in social surveys of charities or to submit full reports of its activities to the State Board of Charity. Guarding its privacy as much as its clients, the Bureau was an insular organization. But even as it defended its recipients publicly, the CCB did seek to influence the people it aided. Specifically, it sought to strengthen their ties to the Church while also encouraging behavior that might win greater "respectability" for Catholics in the larger Protestant-dominated Boston society. Thus, the Bureau criticized alcohol use, illegitimacy, and delinquency among poor families. In the first decades of the twentieth century, the Bureau's use of charity as a means of both defending the Catholic faith and gaining social acceptance for Catholics sparked conflicts since the two goals appeared—and, at times, were—at odds.[14]

Poor women were often caught in the conflicted goals of Catholic charity. The Bureau questioned women who worked outside their homes, and it justified removing children from these homes, citing "absence of the mother." The Bureau's criticism of women working flew in the face of the fact that Massachusetts had a higher than average percentage of women in the workforce, many of them unmarried Irish women. Despite these realities, the Bureau viewed wage work for women a misfortune that should end upon marriage and certainly once children came along. The Bureau supported a strong role for men within families, and it staunchly opposed birth control, divorce, and feminism. Reflecting the conservative position of the church on women's rights, the Bureau sought to reinforce what it considered "traditional" family values, which meant a subservient role for women as dependents and primary caregivers. Individualism, especially for women, was considered a threat to the family.[15]

The tight religious control of the CCB as well as the high turnover rate of its directors limited the interaction of the Bureau with the city's Protestant and Jewish organizations. Unlike the personnel in Protestant agencies, its staff changed nearly completely every three to four years. The Archdiocese had difficulty finding priests interested in working in the charity field and so the Bureau directors—all of whom were priests—changed every four or five years. The CCB staff also changed regularly. The visitors were usually unmarried women who left after only one or two years, probably to marry. Unlike the Protestant and Jewish charities, the CCB did not rely on the volunteer effort of married women, which is not surprising given the Bureau's criticism of married women having responsibilities outside their own homes.

Neither the directors nor their staff had formal training in social work. In fact, they were quite suspicious of professional social work, associating it with Protestants and Protestant ideas. Although their assessment was probably exaggerated, it was not completely untrue. Both on the national level and in Boston, native-born Protestants dominated the emerging profession of social work. Whatever training the Bureau provided, its staff stressed the relationship between their work with the poor and Catholic belief. Only gradually, and with some criticism from their superiors, did the leaders of the CCB become less suspicious of social work theories and begin to work with non-Catholic organizations.[16]

Jewish charity efforts were also consolidated at the turn of the twentieth century, though with less centralized control and much less defensiveness. Boston's comparatively small Jewish population saw the creation of a charity network as a way to strengthen ties among Jewish institutions. In 1895, leaders in the Jewish community established a citywide federation to coordinate Jewish relief efforts through the use of a central exchange. Then in 1908, they founded the Federated Jewish Charities (FJC), which centralized fund-raising for the smaller Jewish charities. As a religiously segregated organization, the Federated established primary aims of assisting Boston's Jewish needy and strengthening the Jewish community through cooperative giving. The rapid influx of Russian and Eastern European Jews around the turn of the century tested the limits of that community. The Federated acted as a bridge between the new and old Jewish groups in Boston, however. Even though its officials remained German Jews, its boards of directors included the leaders of the newer immigrant groups. The Federated brought together older organizations, like the United Hebrew Benevolent Association and the Hebrew Woman's Sewing Society, with new aid societies that Eastern European immigrants had established.[17]

Under lay and not rabbinical leadership, the Federated exhibited greater flexibility and openness than the Catholic Charitable Bureau. The Federated leadership, a combination of businessmen and social workers—men and women—enjoyed a good relationship with public welfare representatives and Protestant social workers. Like the CCB, the Federated campaigned for legislation requiring that Jewish foster children be placed in Jewish homes, but its efforts were less antagonistic. Even before legislation was passed protecting the religious freedom of children, the Federated had little trouble obtaining the names of Jewish children who were wards of the state or permission to move them to Jewish foster homes. As early as the 1880s, the Board of Overseers included a Jewish member and employed a Jewish visitor. Simon E. Hecht, a wealthy wool merchant, joined the Overseers in 1908 and became the Overseers' first Jewish chairman in 1920. Max Mitchell, the Federated's director, attended the White House Conference on Dependent

Children in 1909, a meeting of primarily secular social workers who advocated a larger role for government in provisions for children. The leaders of the Provident and the Associated regarded the work of the Jewish charities favorably and, as a policy, referred Jewish applicants to the Federated.[18]

Even though the Federated fostered good relations with both the Overseers and the leaders of the Protestant charities, it did not share their views on poverty or their critical attitude toward the poor. The Federated, much like the CCB, stressed the environmental causes of poverty. Its main relief agency, the United Hebrew Benevolent Association (UHBA), reported that "insufficient earnings, sickness, and other physical disabilities" accounted for the largest share of the UHBA's cases. Moral weakness, while mentioned, was not a central determinant of poverty, according to the Federated. "Crime and intemperance play but a little part in the sad drama of human lives which is our province to unfold," a Federated report explained in 1912. Like the CCB, the Federated assumed the morality of its recipients or, at least, did not connect immorality to economic hardship.[19]

The Federated, more than the CCB, saw charity as only one part of a larger program to assure economic self-sufficiency. It offered business loans and instituted vocational training programs. Like the Protestant charities, the Federated argued that money alone would not cure poverty; however, its service programs aimed at economic opportunity rather than moral uplift, and the Federated served a broader economic range of families than the other charities in the city. The Federated leaders believed family self-sufficiency was best achieved by insuring employment for the primary male breadwinner. They saw male unemployment—seasonal and long-term—as a particular threat to both family self-sufficiency and to family structure, and they provided business loans and vocational programs to improve the economic opportunities of men with families to support. Although the Federated strove to shore up men's role as heads of households, the Federated leaders did not show the same hostility toward women that the CCB did. Rather than criticizing poor mothers for their wage work or threatening to remove their children, the Federated attempted to assure these women sufficient income and support to avoid wage work. Likewise, it did not condemn the use of birth control or oppose divorce.

The relief programs within the Federated took a more positive approach to charity than either the Protestant or Catholic organization. A sense of justice, more than a sense of pity, informed the work of the Federated. It did not see relief as a potentially corrupting influence, and it offered a higher level of financial support than Boston's other charities. It provided temporary aid during times of family emergency and unemployment and more permanent aid in cases of old age, illness, or widowhood. While its temporary clients received about the same amount of aid as they did from the Overseers, the Federated's permanent clients received up to $25 a week, more than twice the amount that either the Overseers or any other private charity provided in similar cases. The Federated was also less suspicious of the poor. Its policy was to give aid first and to investigate afterward.[20]

The differences among Boston's Protestant, Catholic, and Jewish charities revealed themselves in the practices and policies of these relief agencies, but they were grounded in these charities' ideas about poverty and the poor as well as in their conceptions of family structure and responsibility. Increasing demands on private charitable organizations and growing pressure for an enlarged public welfare program would force these private charities to negotiate their differences.

Public Relief: The Overseers of the Poor

Unlike many American cities, Boston has always operated a poor relief department. Its first board of Overseers of the Poor was assembled in 1691, during the colonial period. Expanded in 1735 to twelve members, the Overseers were required by Massachusetts law to "relieve and support all poor and indigent persons lawfully settled therein." The specifics of how to achieve that goal were left to the localities, however, and Boston's Overseers experimented with a combination of outdoor and indoor relief measures throughout the colonial period and early nineteenth century. In 1864, the Overseers relinquished oversight of certain dependent groups, such as the insane and orphaned children, thus limiting their responsibilities to the outdoor relief program and the administration of temporary shelters for the poor.[21]

During the nineteenth century, the board showed a remarkable continuity of membership and leadership. Native-born men with names like Winthrop, Amory, and Newell served long stints on the board. The directorship changed hands only six times between 1864 and 1918, and the same secretary, Benjamin Pettee, conducted the daily operations of the board for forty years, from 1874 to 1914. In the 1880s and 1890s, however, the board began reflecting social changes in the city. With the election of Boston's first Irish mayor, Hugh O'Brien, in 1884, some men of Irish origin or descent received mayoral appointment to the board. Around the same time, Boston's

Jewish population, then largely of German origin, began to gain representation on the board. In the 1890s, native-born women began to be appointed as Overseers. Diversification, however, brought no fundamental change to the board. Yankee Bostonians remained a majority, and the new members proved accommodating to their leadership.[22]

Though selected by the mayor, the Overseers were understood to be non-political appointments. "Outstanding character" was the most frequent qualification given for appointment to the board; willingness and ability to give freely of one's time as a civic duty also were cited. Meeting on Wednesday afternoons, the board members either did not work or had control over their work schedules. They received no compensation for their time. Despite the board's voluntary foundation, however, the board was a well-defined hierarchical organization. The members of the board chose a chairman from among them and hired a secretary to direct the daily operations of the department. The secretary supervised the staff at the central office and responded to emergency cases, but all executive authority rested in the board and its committees. The secretary directed the work of "district visitors," who interviewed applicants in their homes and investigated their backgrounds. Until the passage of Mothers' Aid in 1913, all of the Overseers' district visitors were men.

The Board of Overseers made all decisions regarding relief. At their weekly meetings, the board heard new cases and reviewed old ones. The district visitors usually presented the information, but occasionally recipients were required to come before the board themselves. The volume of cases discussed usually prohibited lengthy discussion or deliberation concerning individual cases, and all decisions by the board were final.

The guiding philosophy of the Overseers was "economical service to the city," meaning limited public expenditures on the poor. The Overseers were eager to restrict the number of cases on their rolls and granted only the smallest amount of relief, usually in kind. Whenever possible they referred cases to private charities, arguing both that the recipients experienced less shame in accepting private relief and that private charities were better equipped to help the poor. The department's district visitors investigated all new cases, searching for family members or other sources of support that might relieve the city of the case. The department also tightly enforced "settlement," or residency, requirements. While lack of residency did not automatically disqualify cases, it let the city charge either the state or other communities for the relief given to nonresidents. The board believed efforts to "save the city a great deal of money" were the most important function of the department and welcomed any opportunity to limit its expenditures. With a focus on economy, the department did not engage in the then new social work practices. The district visitors gathered only the most basic information about the recipients. The visitors recorded relief dispersal in a single log, making no attempt at casework methodology. The Overseers considered case records, along with the social service that they required, beyond the scope and the budget of the department.[23]

The Overseers restricted most of their aid to widows with children and to old men and women "too feeble to work." Most of the elderly were, in fact, old women, primarily widows whose relatives had died or were unable to care for them. These elderly women were apparently less willing than elderly men to move to the city's old age home on Long Island. In general, elderly women viewed institutional care as more debilitating than their male counterparts. Although half of Boston's elderly women lived alone, they were anxious to stay in their homes in their old age. Destitute and without family support, they relied on the charity of the Overseers.[24]

The Overseers discouraged applications from unemployed men. "The visitors are instructed to refuse aid to all families where there are able-bodied men," stated the 1906 *Annual Report,* "unless the man in the family is willing to work in the wood yard for the aid given." The wood yard was next to the Charity Building, and any man seeking shelter and food at the city's temporary lodging house was required to put in a day's work there, chopping and stacking wood. Associated with vagabonds and drunkards, the wood yard proved a work requirement most unemployed men refused to fulfill. Both the stigma and the small compensation—two days' work in the wood yard entitled a family to a grocery order worth only $2—put most off the idea. The requirement reflected the Poor Law principle of "least eligibility," whereby no relief recipient was to receive more than the lowest market wage. The Overseers of the Poor took great satisfaction in their work requirement and its apparent effectiveness in limiting their relief burden.[25]

Setting up public aid as less desirable and more punitive than private relief, the Overseers maintained their expenditures on a relatively even level. Serving only the most destitute of the city's poor and providing them only enough aid to prevent starvation, the Overseers maintained a budget that represented less than half of 1 percent of the city's operating budget at the beginning of the twentieth century. Public aid was to be limited to cases of dire circumstances for which there seemed no solution or hope.[26]

The limited scope of the municipal poor relief program and the dominance of the city's private relief charities removed the city's charity system from city politics. The Overseers of the Poor seldom, if ever, were called before the City Council or the mayor to explain the workings of their department or to justify their spending. Employing only a small number of people, the public relief department was not a locus for patronage, and the department's limited functions and expenditures offered little opportunity for graft or corruption. Thus, even as the leaders within the charity system engaged in political debates on broader welfare issues, such as workmen's compensation, social insurance, and child welfare, they did not view poor relief, either public or private, as a political concern. But an emerging campaign for a publicly funded widows' pension in Massachusetts would challenge the policies of the public relief department as well as its male leadership. The debates over this new program for poor women and children would also force the private charities to defend their own relief practices. In the process, their differences would become even more pronounced.

2 MOTHERS' AID, 1910–1919

THE CAMPAIGN for a state-funded widows' pension and the eventual passage of the Massachusetts Mothers' Aid Act in 1913 destabilized Boston's charity system. Mounted largely by middle-class women's organizations, the widows' pension movement criticized Boston's public and private relief agencies and proposed a program that would assure an "adequate" income for widowed families by providing public subsidies. The proponents of widows' pensions in Massachusetts, like their counterparts in other states, were motivated both by concern about poor women and children and by anxiety about rapid social changes related to urbanization and immigration. Resenting the criticism of these women's organizations and guarding their control over poor relief, the representatives of the public relief system and the leaders of the Protestant charities blocked the legislation for a widows' pension. In its place, they proposed a Mothers' Aid program over which public welfare officials and Protestant charity leaders would have more control. Passed into law in 1913 and administered by the Overseers of the Poor, Mothers' Aid became a highly supervised relief program for only the poorest women and children.

Despite the efforts by Boston's Protestant charity leaders to limit the impact of this new program, Mothers' Aid developed beyond their control. Its focus on the needs of poor women and children gained strong popular and political support, especially after the election of Massachusetts' first Catholic governor, in 1914. As much a product of the campaign for widows' pensions as of the final legislation, Mothers' Aid broke with traditional poor relief practices by offering a higher level of support to poor women with less of the stigma traditionally associated with public aid. As a result, enrollment in the program soared despite its association with the Overseers of the Poor.

In addition to beginning a shift toward larger public welfare programs and expenditures, Mothers' Aid also offered Boston's Catholic and Jewish charities new opportunities to influence public welfare policy. Unlike the

Protestant charity spokesmen, the leaders of Boston's Catholic and Jewish charities did not oppose the idea of publicly funded widows' pensions and worked with the Mothers' Aid program when it was implemented. The support of Mothers' Aid by Catholic and Jewish charities as well as their increased interaction with the new program weakened the influence of the Protestant charities over the public welfare program. In important ways, then, Mothers' Aid marked a new era in the history of poor relief in Boston.

Historians of social welfare have credited the widows' pensions programs of the Progressive Era with setting the stage for the administrative structure of the welfare programs of the New Deal, and historians of women have investigated the network of women's organizations that campaigned for widows' pension legislation and the experience of Mothers' Aid recipients to uncover the gender assumptions that these welfare programs made about women's dependency and need for supervision. Advancing theories on state capacity for welfare development, historical sociologists have also analyzed these programs for needy mothers. With only a few notable exceptions, scholars have studied Mothers' Aid from a national perspective, an understandable approach since they examine this early public welfare program to understand the origins of the federal welfare programs of the 1930s. The unfortunate result, however, is that the ethnic, racial, and religious conflicts associated with the local campaigns have remained nearly invisible.[1]

The use of the concept of "maternalism" to explain the campaigns for widows' pensions has, likewise, abstracted this welfare reform movement from the local political contexts from which it emerged. "Maternalism" is a malleable concept used by advocates for public assistance to widows with children, as well as by scholars since, to connote the importance of motherhood and the potential unity among women around concerns of mothering. Promoters of this idea argue that the widows' aid movement represented an important recognition of the needs of poor mothers by more privileged mothers, whereas critics insist that maternalism confined poor women, and by implication all women, to socially constructed roles of "fit" or "unfit" mother while offering only limited support to needy families. In either case, focusing on maternalism as a mode of analysis tends to separate the development of welfare policies from the social and cultural conflicts that shape them. In Boston, the advocates of widows' pensions used the rhetoric of maternalism in their campaign for this new public welfare program, but it was that program's connection to existing public relief programs and the various responses of the city's private religious charities that determined its history.[2]

The Campaign

The campaign for widows' pensions in Massachusetts was part of a larger effort nationwide to institute public aid for women and dependent children. Its loudest advocates were women's groups, specifically the National Congress of Mothers and the General Federation of Women's Clubs, whose members were primarily native-born white Protestants from either middle-class or upper middle-class backgrounds. Members of the Women's Trade Union League and the National Consumers' League, settlement house workers, and suffrage leaders also lent support to the effort though it was not their first priority. Poor women joined in the campaign as well, participating at legislative hearings and writing letters to their representatives.[3]

The campaign gained support primarily through the endorsement of women's clubs and discussion in popular women's periodicals, such as *The Delineator*. Because of the campaign's diffused organizational base, the arguments in favor of Mothers' Aid were broadly conceived. All of its advocates stressed the value of women's labor as mothers and the need for public support for needy mothers, but some suggested more radical ideas such as payment to all mothers for bringing up children; others maintained that the primary beneficiaries should be children. Advocates used ideas such as rights, entitlement, duty, and responsibility to support their positions but with no consistency or agreed-upon meaning. Likewise, the wage work of poor mothers was never a settled issue, with some advocates insisting that the pension should remove poor mothers from the labor force while others saw the pension as a wage subsidy.[4]

For three important reasons, however, the movement for widows' pensions did not face the same opposition as other Progressive-era welfare proposals, such as unemployment insurance and old age assistance. First, the widows' pension movement did not challenge gender norms. Its leaders asserted woman's role as the primary caretaker of children and reaffirmed her "dependency" on a male breadwinner, who, in theory at least, earned a "family wage." (That the family wage was an illusion for most poor families did not prevent a construction of gender relations premised on the idealization of men's ability to support their families financially and mothers' need to be dependent on that support.) In the absence of a male breadwinner, women with children could "depend" on public aid without substantially subverting these gender norms, or so it seemed to the proponents of widows' pensions. Unemployment and old age insurance, in contrast, challenged normative gender roles by asserting the need for men to be, at least at times, "dependent." Understood in this way, the movement for Mothers' Aid represented the "conservative wing" of the early twentieth-century women's movement.[5]

Second, as a program for women and children, the widows' pensions did not appear to open the door to corruption and graft, a criticism often leveled at programs for men. Still excluded from the formal political arena, women could not trade votes for public benefits as men were thought capable of doing. Because of this, the widows' pension movement was able to sidestep the Progressive-era obsession over potential abuse of governmental provisions.[6]

Third, the widows' pension movement faced less opposition than other social provision proposals because native-born middle-class women presented these pensions as a means of assuring social stability during a period of intense change. Widows' pensions, unlike other proposals, were advanced not as something new, but, instead, as a means of shoring up the supposedly "traditional" family structure of a male breadwinner with a wife and children as dependents. Moreover, widows' pensions were presented as a social provision program for "better" families, meaning or implying that the very poor and the immigrant were excluded. In many instances, the rhetoric of exclusivity was dashed as immigrant, black, and very poor families looked for support from Mothers' Aid programs, but the initial campaign emphasized the need of middle-class American families for the assurance of widows' pensions.[7]

The Congress of Mothers led the widows' pension campaign in Massachusetts as it did in other states. Founded in 1911, the Massachusetts branch, like the national organization, was an association of native-born white Protestant women. The wives of prominent political, business, and academic leaders, these women enjoyed the financial security and leisure opportunities of upper middle-class and middle-class women of the period. Their activities included statewide conferences on topics related to education, social welfare, and the new field of psychology. Both nationally and locally, the Congress based its authority on the experience of its members, as mothers and took advantage of the atmosphere of increased female political activism to advance their program. From its founding, the Massachusetts Congress of Mothers worked with other women's organizations, such as the Daughters of the American Revolution, the Women's Educational and Industrial Union, the Women's Christian Temperance Union, and the Massachusetts Women's Club. Its founders saw themselves as battling what they called the "well-known conservatism" of Massachusetts regarding both the political role of women and the enlargement of state action.[8]

Clara Cahill Park, a founder and vice president of the Congress in Massachusetts, led the state campaign for widows' subsidies. Originally from the Midwest, Park lived in a suburb of Boston with her four children and husband, Robert E. Park, a leading sociologist. Park had encouraged the organization to sponsor a widowed mother of eight whose struggle to find a suitable house had been published in the local newspapers. The experience convinced Park of the need for a social program for widowed mothers. In 1911, she presented a paper at the Convention of the National Congress of Mothers on "the State and the Fatherless Child." She also met there with others interested in the subject and learned that legislation in Missouri had already been put into place. Returning home, Park spearheaded an aggressive campaign for widows' pensions in Massachusetts.[9]

In battling for widows' aid, spokeswomen for the Congress criticized the practices of public and private relief agencies and the dominance of men in these organizations. They questioned both the amount of support widows received and their treatment by relief officials. Writing in *Home Progress,* a women's magazine, Park described a widow of six, living in a tenement, doing sweatshop homework around the kitchen table with her children. Park contended that "a prominent charity-worker" threatened to remove the children if the mother did not stop taking in homework. He left the house, she reported, "shaking his head over the depravity of mothers." In this vignette and others, Park argued not only that charity workers were uncaring but also that, as men, they could not understand or identify with the double burden of care and support that many mothers faced.[10]

When Park and the Congress invited Rabbi Stephen S. Wise of New York to speak at an evening program on widows' pensions held at the Massachusetts Institute of Technology in January 1913, he, too, criticized the current relief system. He accused private charities of opposing a publicly funded widows' aid program because of their need to use the image of the widowed mother in their fund-raising appeals, adding that, despite their use of the image, they did not adequately aid widows: "Generally speaking, the charity organizations have not been able to bear the burden of adequate maintenance of the widowed mother with her children in their home." The criticism of this outsider did not sit well with the local charity leaders, none of whom accepted invitations to appear with him.[11]

Park and the Mothers' Congress led a grassroots campaign for widows' pensions that positioned the "experts" against the "mothers." Defending the movement for widows' pensions against the criticism of social work leader Edward T. Devine, Park wrote: "You see, mothers, in spite of the sociologists, feel themselves, for once, on their own ground in this matter; and in possession of all their faculties, will continue to think that as far as children are concerned, not they, but the learned doctors, are in the amateur class." She solicited letters from mothers and organized women to petition for legislation. Using the network of local chapters, Park distributed information throughout the state on the legislative campaign for a widows' pension program.[12]

Despite the grassroots organizing style of Parks and the Congress, their campaign for a widows' pension was not truly inclusive. Their program would aid only widows, not mothers who were deserted, divorced, or unmarried. In addition, their proposed plan would cover only "citizens of Massachusetts," thereby excluding all recent immigrants. Repeatedly, Park presented the program as one for "better" mothers who were not receiving public assistance. In a letter sent to women throughout the state, she described the program as one for widows "who are neither unfortunate enough to become objects of charity, nor their needs known because they have made too brave a fight." Elsewhere, Park furthered the distinctions among mothers, arguing that the very poor and the "unfit mother" benefited from state programs while the "capable mother" did not. "When a *good capable* mother comes to the state for help, it passes her on to some private charity, its business being only with the derelict class," wrote Park. Thus, while the maternal rhetoric of the Congress's campaign posited universal motherhood, it limited support to mothers measured as fit and excluded the destitute.[13]

Along with the distinctions among mothers or, perhaps, because of them, the Mothers' Congress stressed the idea of entitlement. "We believe that any widowed mother who has made this good fight is entitled by right to a certain amount of aid in the rearing of her family, which is the foundation of the state," read their circular letter. The well-being of the next generation was at stake, they contended, and the mother should be "recognized as a creditor of the state" while her children were too young to support themselves.[14]

The widows' pension campaign met its strongest opposition from Boston's Protestant charity leadership and members of the State Board of Charity. Viewing the Mothers' Congress as "outsiders" to the charity system, they accused its members of creating sentimental images of widows. They argued that public and private charities could better discriminate among needy widows than a pension program administered by an independent board. In addition, they insisted that the charity system adequately cared for widows despite its division between public and private efforts. Boston's Jewish and Catholic charities did not join the opposition to widows' pensions. Jewish charity leaders saw the proposal for widows' pensions as potentially beneficial to their clients, and, even though they were not part of the Congress of Mothers' campaign, quickly threw their support behind the proposal. The leaders of the Catholic Charitable Bureau were more leery about the potential benefit of a widows' pension program. Initially, they expressed concern that such a program might increase the power of the state over poor Catholic women. CCB officials viewed the state, accurately so at the time, as the Protestant establishment. Despite their reservations, the CCB leaders did not lobby against the widows' pensions nor did they join the Protestant charity leaders in attacking the proposal.[15]

Thus, the dispute over widows' pensions was not simply a battle between private and public charities. The Protestant charity leaders strongly opposed the widows' aid proposal because it had the potential to weaken their influence over the charity system. Moreover, by singling out widows with children, the proposed program ran counter to the Protestant charity leaders' philosophy of individual responsibility and accountability and infringed on their prerogative to determine the eligibility and "worthiness" of each relief case. Boston's Jewish and Catholic charities, smaller and with less influence over the public welfare program, particularly at the state level, were not as threatened by the widows' pension proposal. Furthermore, the campaign's emphasis on family unity and women's dependence complemented the perspectives on family structure and gender roles of the Jewish and Catholic charity leaders. Nevertheless, because of the dominance of the larger Protestant charities in Boston and on the national level, the legislative debate of widows' pension did, in fact, become a battle between the Protestant charity establishment and the advocates of widows' pensions. As campaign gave way to legislation and legislation to implementation, Catholic and Jewish charity leaders began to play an increasingly influential role in the unfolding of this new public welfare program.[16]

Legislative Process

In May 1912, with the cooperation of the General Federation of Women's Clubs and the endorsement of Boston lawyer and future Supreme Court justice Louis Brandeis, Park and the Congress succeeded in having legislation passed that set up a commission to study the need for a widows' pension. Governor Eugene Foss, a Democrat who championed Progressive issues, appointed Robert F. Forester, Harvard professor of social ethics; David F. Tilley, member of the State Board of Charity and former member of the Central Council of the Society of St. Vincent de Paul; and Clara Cahill Park to study the issue. The commission was given space at the statehouse, and over the next six months it conducted hearings and surveyed public and private charities. During the course of its work, the dire poverty of widows, native-born and immigrant alike, came into focus.[17]

The commission solicited the testimony of poor women throughout the state. Transcripts of these hearings do not exist, but the testimony of one widow, reported in a Boston newspaper, suggested both the difficulties poor mothers faced and, sadly, their lack of understanding about the widows' pensions proposal. The widow, Camella Torpia, lived in Boston's congested North End neighborhood. Using an interpreter, she explained that her husband had died two years earlier, leaving her with four children to support. At first she relied on a private charity, but its $2 a week in groceries did not go very far. With the children constantly sick, the State Board of Charity took the three oldest away, boarding them first in New Hampshire and then in Lowell, a city near Boston. There, Mrs. Torpia had visited them whenever possible, although she was having increasing difficulty communicating with them since she spoke only Italian and her children were quickly losing their Italian after being away from home for nearly two years. Recently, the boys had been moved again but no notification had been given to their mother. Weeping and pleading before the legislative committee, Mrs. Torpia was the perfect witness for widows' pensions. Although her interpreter, a woman social worker from the Italian Mission, connected Mrs. Torpia's plight to Massachusetts' lack of a pension for widows, Mrs. Torpia did not mention pensions in her testimony. In fact, she had come before the committee thinking that the senators and representatives could somehow return her children to her, and urged her interpreter to "put the case as strongly as possible." Members of the Mothers' Congress had recruited Mrs. Torpia, thinking her story particularly moving, but evidently failed to explain to her the purpose of the hearing. This episode suggests that the movement for widows' pensions was more a movement for poor women than by poor women.[18]

Despite the efforts of the Mothers' Congress, the commission issued a divided report in January 1913. The majority report, written by Forester and Park, indicted public and private charities for their inadequate response to the needs of widows with children. Citing the commission's survey of public and private charities, the report said that in half the cases in which children were separated from their widowed mothers, financial hardship was the cause. The report argued that poor widows were losing their children to orphanages and foster homes for lack of sufficient income or because of need to work outside their homes. Widows' subsidies, it concluded, would prevent the separation of children from their mothers.[19]

While not noted by Forester and Park, the survey findings had been significantly influenced by information from Boston's Jewish and Catholic charities. In the survey, these charities had overwhelmingly given "economics" as the reason for family separation, refusing to comment publicly on the personal characteristics of their recipients. The Protestant charity leaders, who seldom or never identified economics as a sole cause for the difficulties of the poor, had cited economics as only one of many difficulties faced by poor widows who had lost their children. Nevertheless, that inclusion of economics as a possible explanation along with the Catholic and Jewish reporting of economic difficulties in nearly every case allowed the majority members to argue that widows were losing their children to orphanages through no fault of their own.[20]

Park and Forester contended that private charities provided too little financial support to widows to prevent the breakup of families. According to Park and Forester, those who were able to keep their children relied primarily on their own wages and on wages of older children to maintain their families. Since both the type of work, mostly domestic and personal service, and the amount of work, usually part-time, offered meager wages, these poor women often had to compensate by taking in lodgers, doing laundry, and engaging in homework. Charity, Parker and Forester said, came only after these other means of support and usually provided even less. The piecing together of wages, charity, and informal sources of support—the longtime strategy of survival by poor women with children—was being called into question.[21]

A uniform, publicly funded aid program of "subsidies for children of indigent widows" was the solution to the problems faced by widowed mothers, according to Forester and Park. The subsidy would not necessarily exempt a widow from wage work, but the intention was to make wage work less necessary for widows with children, particularly very young children. A separate commission appointed by the governor would administer the program, and neither the local Overseers of the Poor nor the State Board of Charity would determine or supervise its activities. The local Overseers of the Poor would distribute the funds, as determined by the special commission and by special field agents employed by the commission. The state would refund one-third of the cost of the subsidies for families with settlement and two-thirds of the cost for those without settlement.

Forester and Park's proposal represented a strike against the charity system already in place. The proposal endeavored to free the widows' subsidy program from any control by the State Board of Charity, whose members opposed the idea, even as it stipulated that the state fund the subsidy. Reflecting its origin among women activists, the proposal reserved two positions on the widows' subsidy board for women and exempted its staff from civil service requirements. The consequence of these stipulations would be a relief program outside the control of the predominately male charity leadership.

To remove widows' subsidies even further from traditional poor relief, the proposal attached certain requirements to the payments of widows' subsidies, all of which countered long-established poor relief practices in Massachusetts. First, the widows' subsidies program required a grant that would let the family reach "a suitable standard of living." No set amount was specified or guaranteed, but the proposal intended for widows' subsidies to be larger than the current grants to widows by the Overseers. Its stipulation of "adequate" funding was a reaction against the practice, common among public relief and private Protestant agencies, of providing less than what was needed. Second, the plan prohibited the Overseers from relying on private charities to aid widowed families, ending the century-old practice of looking to private charities to keep public costs down. Third, the proposal protected widows' subsidy recipients from being categorized as paupers, a legal status then attached to all public poor relief cases. As much as it outlined the practices of the proposed subsidies program, the majority report distinguished the new plan from older forms of charities.

The proposed subsidies program included eligibility restrictions that also distinguished the new plan from traditional poor relief. Only widows with minor children would be considered for support, and non-citizens would be excluded. In addition, eligible widows had to demonstrate that they were worthy and "capable of expending money for the true interests of the children" and provide a home environment that the commission found "desirable." Morality tests had been attached to poor relief earlier, but none had specifically identified mothering skills as a measure of worthiness. The

Overseers or members of the commission would visit the recipients' homes three times a year to determine the family's suitability. Forester and Park argued that the proposal's restrictions helped ensure that the widows' subsidies program would be "not primarily for those with least adequate incomes under the present system of aid, but for the fit and the worthy poor." Thus, even as the majority cited the economic difficulties of all widowed families, it proposed a program in keeping with the campaign by the Mothers' Congress for a more selective program aimed at native-born widows who could prove their "fitness" for support.[22]

In the minority report, David F. Tilley contended that the commission's study and recommendations were flawed. As a member of the State Board of Charity, Tilley opposed the creation of a new and independent board for widows' subsidies. He defended the state's poor relief system, arguing that it was "different from most other States." Relief laws in Massachusetts, he said, were "broad enough, if properly applied, to provide adequately for all classes—widows, widowers, mothers with sick husbands, etc."[23]

Leaders of Boston's Protestant charities pointed to Tilley's dissent as evidence of the commission's divided conclusions, but he acted neither as their representative nor did he share all of their objections to the proposed program. In his minority report, Tilley suggested that the new program would increase state expenses, an opinion that the programs' leading opponents shared. Tilley departed, however, from the standard fiscally conservative argument of the Protestant charity leadership by adding: "We need . . . a liberal interpretation of our existing statutes and a realization on the part of our different communities that those who are elected or appointed to serve them as overseers of the poor are not selected because of their ability to keep the tax rate down, but because of their ability to do what is best for those who, through no fault of their own, have become dependent upon public charity." Tilley's assertion that the poor were dependent "through no fault of their own" was not in keeping with the leading Protestant charities' philosophy nor was his criticism of some boards of Overseers for their fiscal conservatism. His criticism of the Overseers as well as his defense of the poor reflected his own background in Boston's Catholic charities and his belief that public charity should be less punitive and restrictive. Nevertheless, Tilley's refusal to support the commission's findings and its proposed bill became the platform for the leaders of the Boston's Protestant charities as they endeavored to defeat the commission's proposed legislation.[24]

Several of the leading Protestant charities disputed the findings of the survey and the way Forester and Park used the survey to criticize them. They defended their removal of children, contending that the economic difficulties of families were usually coupled with moral deficiencies. Falling back on their individualistic philosophy, these charity leaders argued that removing children from their homes gave their mothers the opportunity to earn a living and to contribute to their children's support, gaining "self-respect" in the process. One charity even insisted that these mothers would refuse a pension even if one were offered, preferring to support themselves and their children through wage work.[25]

Boston's Jewish and Catholic charities did not criticize the commission's report and supported the majority report's focus on the economic difficulties of poor mothers. Louis Cohen of the Home for Jewish Children stated that some of the children in the Home could be kept in their own homes if their mothers were aided "regularly and surely." He continued: "If the financial head, or father, is taken from his children, the mother, if a proper person, can still guide and keep her children if she can obtain a certain sum that she may depend upon regularly." The charities, he asserted, did not have "sufficient funds to carry the work to its proper scope." Likewise, Sister Rose of the St. Vincent Orphan Asylum supported the idea of a steady income source for mothers with children. "Could the family be maintained under the eye of the mother by charity, no matter from what source, private or public, the results would be much more to the purpose." Father Michael J. Scanlan, director of the Catholic Charitable Bureau, also registered the Bureau's opposition to family separation; however, he appeared less enthusiastic about the commission's proposal for uniform support favoring, instead, the boarding out of poor children at Catholic orphanages.[26]

The commission's report and the charities' reactions to it sparked little interest in the general public, but in social work periodicals, such as *The Survey*, the Massachusetts proposal was highlighted and debated. Those in the social work and charity fields recognized that this program, though small, had the potential to set precedents in relief policy. Boston's Protestant charity leaders, many whom regularly contributed to these periodicals, attacked the proposal and defended their work with the poor. Their complaints focused on three issues. First, they doubted the commission's "real" experience working with poor people. "To determine just where [the failure of relief] does lie," wrote one critic, "calls for a study requiring money, time, and the sure touch of somebody who knows what to look for." According to this critic, the commission's study and mothers' pension "schemes" in other states fell short of this. The Protestant charity leaders also contended that the commission, as well as the women's groups behind the plan, "romanticize the poor widow." A categorical subsidy, they believed, would not sufficiently differentiate among widows. In their opinion, "The cause of the husband's death [was] not always a satisfactory test of a wife's moral habits." In addition, the Protestant leaders criticized the commission's proposed legislation for not including all poor mothers. They attacked the commission for suggesting that other groups of poor people should be left at the mercy of public and private relief, programs that the commission dismissed as incompetent and inadequate.[27]

How do we interpret the reaction against the widows' subsidies proposal by Boston's Protestant charity network? At the core, these charity leaders were offended by the criticism of their relief programs and of their informal cooperation with public relief officials. While their claim to having more experience with poor women than some of the proponents of the plan was probably true, their defensiveness primarily concerned the potential of the widows' subsidies program to weaken their influence over poor relief policy. That the proposal had been spearheaded by a women's organization and that the leadership of the private charity organization was largely male furthered the differences between the two camps, though women in the Protestant charity network also attacked the widows' subsidies program. Their attack on the proposal for its restriction to widows, which they described as elitist, was primarily a defense of the current charity system and the prerogative it gave them to determine eligibility for poor relief on a case by case basis.

Despite the criticism of the Protestant charity leaders, the majority members of the commission and supporters of the new legislation remained committed to it. They stood by its conclusion that widows with children were not adequately supported by public and private charity. To the charge that the proposed program ignored the needs of other poor people, Forester and Park remained firm in their conviction of a need for a special program for widowed mothers. The new program, they conjectured, could set new standards for other poor relief programs, arguing that, although restricted to widows, the subsidies program represented "the entering wedge of a system of state endowment of motherhood." Park worked the network of women's clubs to generate support for the commission's bill, prompting petitions and letters to the state legislature.[28]

Recognizing the likelihood that the "subsidies bill" would become law, the leaders of Boston's Protestant charities joined forces to propose an alternative bill. Alice Higgins, general secretary of the Associated Charities, was behind this effort, recognizing sooner than the other Protestant charity leaders that the Mothers' Congress and other women's groups were close to success in shaping social welfare legislation despite their lack of practical experience in the charity field. "This movement will mean a new law in this state," she reportedly said. "If those who understand family social work do not guide it, the result may be wholly inconsistent with the principles of our social legislation. Let us take a part."[29]

To maintain the charity system as they saw it, Boston's Protestant charity leaders met in the offices of the Boston Provident Association and drafted a bill, known then as the "social workers' Mothers' Aid bill." The authors of this bill included the directors of Boston's Protestant relief agencies as well as leaders from other Protestant-led children's aid and protection agencies, such as the Children's Aid Society and the Massachusetts Society for the Prevention of Cruelty to Children. These charity leaders acted swiftly and privately to block passage of the subsidies bill. Using their connections with leaders in the state legislature, they succeeded in having their alternative bill, referred to as the social workers' bill, forwarded to the Committee on Social Welfare along with the commission's bill. William Pear, the general secretary of the Provident Association, appeared before the committee in February. He pressed for passage of the social workers' bill, citing its application to all poor women and criticizing the commission's idea of setting up a new governing body to administer the new program. The best program, Pear insisted, was one locally administered even if partially funded by state moneys. The committee was convinced and returned a bill that was in all regards the same as the social workers' proposal; it became law on June 12, 1913.[30]

The Mothers' Aid Act was less restrictive than the widows' aid proposal in that it included all mothers, not only widows, and it did not exclude noncitizens. However, it was more conservative in its greater emphasis on supervision. The Mothers' Aid Act required elaborate record keeping on each family and home visits at least four times a year. The expansion of the program to all mothers and its stronger supervisory component were connected since, in the minds of these social workers and charity leaders, a larger pool of potential applicants would require more administration and evaluation. Unlike the commission's proposal, the Mothers' Aid Act did not set up an independent board to administer the aid, but, instead, used the local Overseers of the Poor, under the supervision of the State Board of Charity. Additionally, as the leaders of the Protestant private charities had insisted, the bill did not prohibit private charities from contributing to the support of poor mothers.

Yet, even as the social workers' bill cast Mothers' Aid as a "relief" program and not an entitlement, its measures included at least some of the features of the commission's bill. Like the commission's bill, the legislation required that Mothers' Aid ensure the "adequate" support of mothers with dependent children, and it noted that Mothers' Aid recipients should be distinguished from other recipients of poor relief by not being categorized as paupers. In addition, although the local Overseers of the Poor administered the Mothers' Aid program, a Mothers' Aid department at the state level, staffed by women, would supervise their work. These concessions demonstrated the success of the widows' pension movement in pressuring the charity establishment into action and greater generosity. Likewise, the establishment of a Mothers' Aid department answered the demands for female leadership in the poor relief program. These features of the Mothers' Aid Act would significantly influence the implementation of Mothers' Aid and its impact on other public relief programs.

Implementation

With the defeat of the commission's "widows' subsidies" bill, the Massachusetts Congress of Mothers retreated from the issue, shifting its focus to parent-teacher programs and activities geared more closely to its middle-class membership. Scholars have connected the retreat of women's organizations from the issue of Mothers' Aid to the general "waning of maternalism," a cession of political action in the interest of mothers by women, many of them mothers themselves. Whether celebratory or critical of the politics of maternalism, these scholars generally see the retreat of women's organizations from welfare issues as an unfortunate development that left programs like Mothers' Aid chronically underfunded and in the hands of less "caring" social workers. The implementation of Mothers' Aid in Boston, however, suggests that this view of early twentieth-century welfare policy is only partially correct. In Boston, the retreat of women's organizations from the issue of Mothers' Aid and the success of the Protestant charity establishment in determining the initial shape of this program planted the Mothers' Aid program within the existing charity system, but as the program grew and the political environment in Boston and at the state level changed, this new welfare program uprooted the city's nineteenth-century charity system.[31]

Nonetheless, during its first year of implementation, Mothers' Aid was primarily under control of native-born men and women who shared the outlook of the Protestant charity leadership in Boston. Ada Sheffield, a long-time member of the State Board of Charity and former Associated Charities worker, directed the new department. Emma W. Lee, "a woman of large experience in charitable work," oversaw the daily operations of the program and supervised the staff of five women visitors.[32]

The new Mothers' Aid department acted quickly to counteract any persisting impression that the new program promised an entitlement. Writing in 1913, the state's director of relief commented: "It is to be regretted that the agitation for so-called widows' pension should have become so fixed in the public mind that the present law is looked upon as a pension act or annuity rather than a relief measure." In response, the Charity Board and the Mothers' Aid department set policies to make sure that Mothers' Aid was seen as "relief" and not an entitlement. Specifically, the state set up a means test that limited the cash and real estate a recipient could hold, and it prohibited the recipients, much as it prohibited poor relief cases, from buying insurance. These policies assured that only the poorest families could qualify for the program. As a result, Mothers' Aid quickly took on the characteristics of public poor relief: its enrollment became restrictive and its assistance limited.[33]

Moreover, while the Mothers' Aid bill had stipulated aid to all poor mothers, the Mothers' Aid department excluded mothers with only one child and all unmarried mothers. The administrators of the new program believed that mothers with only one child should depend on the support of relatives and private charities or be self-supporting through wage work. They excluded unmarried mothers on "moral" grounds. To aid unmarried mothers, explained Sheffield, "would offend the moral feeling of respectable mothers and would thus do violence to a traditional sentiment that is inseparable from a respect for virtue." The concern about respectability led the department unofficially to favor applications from widows over those from women who had been deserted, divorced, or separated. Among the small numbers of deserted, divorced, or separated cases, called "women with irresponsible husbands" to remove any taint of blame toward the women, the department aided more women who had been deserted than those divorced or separated. A 1918 study of the program indicated that 73 percent of the cases in Boston were widowed families, while 14 percent of the cases were families in which the husband was incapacitated, and 13 percent of the cases involved desertion, divorce, or separation. Finally, the department prohibited aiding mothers who took in male boarders; despite the financial benefit of this household arrangement, the Mothers' Aid department considered these men "an influence making toward an unfit home." Boston's Protestant charities had long expressed a similar disapproval of boarders and considered them a potential sexual threat or temptation to women. The new Mothers' Aid program was being crafted along the regulatory lines of the Protestant charity establishment.[34]

Under Sheffield's direction, the policy of the Mothers' Aid department was to supplement and not supplant income from other sources. In calculating the "income" of families, the state board included money from a number of sources, including pensions, relatives, wages of the mother and older children, and private societies. It then deducted the families' incomes from their expenses to determine the grant. As was the practice among Protestant charities, the Mothers' Aid program encouraged women to engage in wage work, associating it with the mothers' need for independence and the value of her actively supporting her family. Mothers were not encouraged to discontinue wage working unless their health was impaired or their children required more personal supervision. Justifying the policy, Sheffield explained, "To insist that the mother shall not work, regardless of home conditions, would tend to discourage that desire for thrift and independence which is an essential element in society." The work requirement reduced the expense of the program and established Mothers' Aid as a source of partial support, similar to traditional poor relief. As a consequence, the department did not set a base income level in determining grants but, instead, left it to the discretion of the visitors. The department recommended that the visitors consider "the former income, and the former standards of living of the family, as well as the standards of self-supporting citizens in the neighborhood" in determining a family's grant. These policies assured, even celebrated, the caseworker's subjectivity in assessing a family's need, a subjectivity characteristic of traditional poor relief but which now was being justified in terms of social work methodology.[35]

Aspects of the Mothers' Aid program were, in fact, even more restrictive and intrusive than traditional poor relief. The new program demanded quarterly inspections of the recipients' homes and more thorough investigations of their backgrounds than general poor relief had required. One Boston case study, for example, described a "Mrs. K.," a Polish woman deserted by her husband; she was visited thirteen times during a four-month period by state Mothers' Aid social workers concerned about her cooking and housekeeping skills. Writing about the new program, Ada Sheffield praised the "regulative value of relief," comparing it to the work of police departments and prisons. It is not insignificant that the regulatory aspect of relief was applied so enthusiastically to a program for women—and one administered by women. As implemented, Mothers' Aid was an example of what the historian Linda Gordon has called "coercive maternalism." Its administrators posited that poor women, perhaps even more than poor men, needed supervision and guidance, and the administrators saw women social workers as best fit for this supervisory role. Through operating much like other "paternalistic" welfare measures, the maternalism of the Mothers' Aid program was grounded in the subordination of women and the identification of women primarily as mothers.[36]

When a woman applied for Mothers' Aid, she immediately confronted its more onerous bureaucratic requirements. First she filled out an application at the Overseers office. In Boston, this meant a trip downtown to the headquarters on Hawkins Street. A visitor from the Overseers, usually a man, then interviewed the woman in her home and investigated her background. Next, the visitor checked public records on the family's births, deaths, and marriages and determined whether the family had settlement in Boston or in another city or town. If the visitor was convinced of the family's need, he presented the case to the Board of Overseers at their weekly meeting. If the board granted the aid, the woman's record was reported to the Mothers' Aid department of the State Board of Charity. A state Mothers' Aid visitor, always a woman, then made another investigation of the family. In many ways, her investigation duplicated the first investigation; the state visitor contacted public and private agencies that might be aiding the family, sought out relatives, and verified family information through public documents. The state visitor then wrote a report on the family. This report was more detailed than the Overseers' report, including the employment activities of the mother and children, school grades, and health. Based on the report, the state visitor estimated the family budget and determined the grant size. The state supervisor of the Mothers' Aid program reviewed the material with the state worker and made the final determination. Her recommendation then had to be approved by the director of the division of aid and relief of the State Board of Charity.

A higher grant level accompanied the increased level of regulation and was often used to justify the intensive supervision of cases. Even when calculated against other sources of income, from relatives, charities, and wage work, the Mothers' Aid grant averaged $10 a week, a dramatic increase over the traditional $2 a week the Overseers provided and higher than grants from most private charities. The higher level of support separated Mothers' Aid from the meagerness of traditional poor relief, but more important, it introduced the idea of fully meeting a family's financial need.

Because of the higher levels of aid, poor mothers enrolled in the Mothers' Aid program despite its burdensome requirements and the intrusiveness of its social workers. During its first month, the new program funded 1,150 mothers with children, 40 percent of them from Boston. Women who had never used public aid before applied to the program; meanwhile, Overseers throughout the state began shifting cases to the new program to take advantage of the one-third state reimbursement, and private charities, particularly Jewish charities, encouraged poor mothers on their rolls to apply. Immigrants made up more than half the cases, with Irish, Russian, and Italian families constituting the largest groups of "foreign-born" cases in Boston.[37]

Over the next six years, Mothers' Aid became the largest and most expensive relief program in the city's history, aiding 1,602 families at an expense of $586,341 in 1919. This represented an explosion in the use of public welfare; by comparison, in 1910 the Boston public aid caseload, including not only needy mothers but also the aged poor, indigent, ill, and unemployed, had totaled only 1,995 families and cost only $83,737. The total expenditures on the Mothers' Aid program more than doubled between its first full year of operation, 1914, and 1919. During the same time, the enrollment and expenditures on the Mothers' Aid program far exceeded the expenditures on all other public relief, now called "Dependent Aid." Providing primarily for the city's destitute elderly and ill, as well as for some mothers who did not qualify for Mothers' Aid, Dependent Aid was dwarfed by the growth of Mothers' Aid.[38]

The expansion of Mothers' Aid was not exempt from political shifts occurring in Massachusetts. In 1914, the state's first Irish-Catholic governor, David I. Walsh, was elected. Walsh's victory ended Yankee Republican control of the state government and opened new opportunities for Catholics in state politics and administration. Over the protest of the Protestant charity network, Walsh did not reappoint Ada Sheffield to the Board of Charity, thus ending control of the Mothers' Aid program by the Protestant private charity network. In Sheffield's place, Elizabeth Moloney, a Catholic woman, was hired to supervise the Mothers' Aid department. While little personal information is known about Moloney, it is clear that she operated outside the Protestant charity establishment, and she opened the Mothers' Aid department to other outsiders, hiring young Catholic women as visitors.[39]

Moloney's public reports suggest that she viewed the Mothers' Aid program in broader terms than its originators and first administrators had. She saw Mothers' Aid not only as a relief program for women but also as a program with more generous grants and services that might influence the enlargement of other public relief programs. Speaking at a conference on Mothers' Aid sponsored by the Children's Bureau in 1922, Moloney recast the history of the Mothers' Aid Act in Massachusetts as she set her own philosophy on the program: "Those who framed the law had in mind two distinct purposes: first, to prevent the breaking up of the homes of fatherless families; and second, to raise the level of public relief. Of the two purposes, that of raising the level of public relief was the more important and far-reaching." Moloney contended that the introduction of Mothers' Aid had forced the Overseers to determine family budgets and that they had begun to apply that practice to all of their cases. This practice, according to Moloney, was pushing the Overseers to enlarge their poor relief grants beyond the traditional $2 or $3 weekly allowance. In reality, those who had drafted the Mothers' Aid legislation had not intended to "raise the level of public relief" but to be sure that expenses were controlled. In contrast, Moloney saw Mothers' Aid as a "wedge" to more generous poor relief for all public cases.[40]

Moloney enthusiastically supported the program and the women who benefited from it. She insisted that the visitors respect the wishes of the mothers and include them in decisions about their families. On this she wrote: "The mother's advice and preference should be given due consideration. Unless she understands and accepts the plan as a reasonable and proper rule of living, her cooperation and support in following out the plan cannot be expected." More than her predecessors, she sought to engage mothers, not merely to regulate them.[41]

Moloney often used case studies to demonstrate how mothers had improved their lives because of Mothers' Aid. The Protestant charities had long used cases studies to illustrate their work, and the Children's Bureau, established at the federal level in 1923, continued this practice in its many studies of local programs of aid to mothers with dependent children. However, unlike those case studies, Moloney's focused on the families, not on the social workers. Although Moloney's accounts describe the work of her department, she was more concerned about defending the poor than the new profession of social work. She stressed, for example, how the financial support of the program, and not merely its supervisory role, made it a route out of poverty for some families. "Mr. and Mrs. O," according to Moloney, lived with their eight children in three rooms in a tenement house in Boston's North End, a congested area crowded with recent Italian immigrants. Mr. O, an Italian laborer suffering from advanced tuberculosis, had been sent to the hospital. Mrs. O then applied for aid from the Boston Overseers. Initially, the local Overseers granted her $12 a week under the Mothers' Aid program, but the state board recommended that the grant be set at $18 a week. Enrolled in the program, this family, according to Moloney, benefited not only from the financial security of a regular and comparatively generous grant, but also from the coordinated effort of public and private health and charity associations, which found the family a new home on the outskirts of the city. "Soon the effects of better housing conditions, close health supervision, and increased aid began to show in the improved health of the entire family." Some of the older children found work, and the younger children enrolled in school. As the children reached working age and found employment, the aid was reduced until it was wholly withdrawn after four years and three months. Moloney recounted the educational and employment success of the oldest children: one graduated from evening high school courses and worked in a railroad office, a second took university extension courses and was a draftsman making $7 a day, a third worked for the Hood Rubber Company, earning $18 a week, and the oldest daughter earned $20 a week running a power machine in an underwear factory. Moloney concluded: "This family is healthy, happy and prosperous, thanks to the timely help which the State and city provided for them in their time of need." No mention was made of the mother working or needing wage work to gain self-respect.[42]

In this and other case studies, Moloney expressed a belief in the goodness of public aid and recipients of public aid, a sentiment not typical of her Protestant counterparts. She did not lobby to enlarge the program to unmarried mothers—something the legislation restricted—but pushed to enlarge benefits for women who were eligible for the program. In her campaign, she expressed little concern about the moral worth of the poor and even admitted the difficulty of determining "fitness" among the applicants to the program. She shared none of the fears about the supposed debilitating effects of public dependency that pervaded the Protestant social work network, nor did she stress the need for poor mothers to work. Instead, she presented public aid as a means for the poor to improve their lives over a period of time, during which they would be dependent on the aid.[43]

Given the new administration and higher cost of Mothers' Aid, the program met some resistance from Boston's Overseers of the Poor. Still dominated by native-born men with ties to business or to the Protestant charities, the Overseers questioned the potential cost of the program. Much to the dismay of the Overseers, the state's Mothers' Aid department seemed intent on making sure that the program's promise of "adequate" support was kept. In many cases, the state visitors recommended a higher grant than originally determined by the local visitors, and, if the locality refused to increase its grant, the state board refused to reimburse the state's one-third share. The Overseers resented the control that the Mothers' Aid department exerted over their operations.[44]

The Overseers were also critical of the Mothers' Aid program because it was directed and staffed by women. The Overseers' staff of older men had difficulty working with the visitors from the Mothers' Aid department. Calling them "a group of comparatively inexperienced young women," the Overseers complained that the visitors from the Mothers' Aid department often recommended a higher grant level than the Overseers, who were used to the lower grants of traditional poor relief. They described the differences between their male visitors and the female Mothers' Aid visitors: "These young women were very positive in their statements of the conditions and needs of the families visited and were upheld as a rule by the State Board, even when opposed by the judgement of experienced overseers of the poor. It is unfortunate in many ways that there would be the necessity of accounting between different boards with somewhat diverse interests, and it seems especially unfortunate that proper consideration should not be given to the opinions of experienced men of mature years." In short, new standards, new practices, and new female social workers challenged the tradition of poor relief in Boston, a system long administered by a staff of men with the sole prerogative to determine the needs of poor families.[45]

The leaders of Boston's Protestant charities, with their own staffs of "female visitors" and ties to the emerging field of social work, were less critical of Mothers' Aid as a program administered by women, but they shared the Overseers' concern about the increased public expenditures on Mothers' Aid. Although leaders of the Protestant charities had joined with other social workers in drafting the Mothers' Aid Act, the program's growing enrollment and expenditures—and likely its supervision by a Catholic woman—prompted objections from them. They argued that the program would result in "considerable cost" to taxpayers, and they objected to what one leader described as the "danger" of "unwarranted satisfaction derived from mere statements of the number of mothers helped and the amount of money involved."[46]

In addition to citing fiscal concerns, the leaders of the largest Protestant agencies contended that Mothers' Aid weakened individual responsibility and self-sufficiency. William Pear of the Boston Provident Association argued that preventative measures based on individual behavior were better social welfare plans. As implemented, the Mothers' Aid program in Massachusetts, particularly in Boston, was providing large enough grants to lessen the need for wage work or private charity. As the expenses of the new program mushroomed, and as the size of its grants began outstripping the support provided by similar programs in other states, Pear sought to disassociate himself with the program; in fact, he claimed he had only reluctantly participated in the drafting of the "social workers' Mothers' Aid bill." He argued that other legislation, such as the 1911 Workmen's Compensation bill that he had also helped to draft, could better protect families from poverty. He insisted that Workmen's Compensation was a "more fundamental claim" than Mothers' Aid because, in his mind, the former was based on the work of an individual, the male breadwinner, and not on the woman's status as a mother. The labor of mothers within the household did not represent work to Pear. The leaders of the Associated Charities, likewise, warned against the "debilitating" effects of public dependency. "Dependency," they argued, fostered laziness and a sense of entitlement. These effects offset any positive impact the program might have in keeping children with their mothers, they said. Mothers, like all individuals, they believed, should strive to support their families through individual effort. State aid, they insisted, should only supplement that effort.[47]

The city's Jewish and Catholic charities shared none of these reservations about the Mothers' Aid program. During the campaign and legislative battle, they had supported a publicly funded program for needy mothers and widows. Under the direction of Martha Silverman, the Federated Jewish Charities immediately transferred their widows' pension cases to the public welfare department, much to the objection of the Overseers. Silverman worked out an arrangement with the Overseers so visitors from the Federated could continue working with Jewish families on Mothers' Aid and even supplement Mothers' Aid payments at times. The combination of public and private grants would assure these Jewish families full support, removing the need for wage work for mothers. Writing in 1919, the Federated's Welfare Committee applauded Mothers' Aid, saying that Jewish recipients within the program had benefited from the legislation.[48]

The Catholic Charitable Bureau, in contrast, was initially worried that a Mothers' Aid program might increase the ability of public officials to supervise needy Catholic families. By 1915, however, the CCB had become more supportive of the new program. The popularity of the program may have swayed the Bureau's opinion, but the more likely explanation was Moloney's appointment as supervisor of the state's Mothers' Aid department. While there is no evidence that Moloney had any direct relationship to the CCB, her appointment appears to have assured the Bureau that Protestants did not control the Mothers' Aid program, as they did the State Board of Charity. Commenting on the program in 1922, the Bureau's director credited the Mothers' Aid program for providing the financial support to keep children with their mothers and, specifically, to keep Catholic children in Catholic homes. Like the Jewish charity leaders, the CCB's officials did not advocate wage work for mothers on public assistance. The value of wage work for poor mothers, whether as a source of self-respect or family support, was not argued, and the dependency of both mother and children was assumed.[49]

Thus, although the representatives of the Protestant charities were able to influence the drafting of the Mothers' Aid legislation and its early policies, the program got away from them. The fiscal expansion of the program as well as an increase in Catholic Democratic power at the state level weakened the influence of Protestant charities on this new public welfare program. Under the direction of Elizabeth Moloney and with the support of Jewish and Catholic charity leaders, the Massachusetts Mothers' Aid set higher standards of "adequate support" for poor mothers and did not insist on wage work for mothers. Unlike their Protestant counterparts, Catholic and

Jewish leaders did not disparage dependency, and they sought to disassociate public poor relief and pauperism. During the next decade, the expansion of public welfare, begun with the Mothers' Aid program, would continue. However, the politics surrounding that expansion would set new priorities that would overshadow Mothers' Aid.

3 POLITICS AND PUBLIC WELFARE, 1920–1929

P UBLIC POOR relief entered the fray of municipal politics in Boston during the 1920s. Mayors and city councilmen discussed poor relief policy as they never had previously, and for the first time, the city's welfare program was debated within a democratic forum. By and large, the debate divided along ethnic lines. A mixed assortment of Irish politicians, by no means allies, began to champion the cause of the city's poor. Claiming to speak for all poor ethnic groups, they demanded an enlarged and politically accountable public welfare program. In contrast, Yankee politicians associated increases in public welfare spending with political corruption and patronage. In order to curb welfare expenditures and to reaffirm their political control over poor relief, they wanted to remove welfare policymaking from the democratic arena where Irish politicians enjoyed the majority. These contesting political agendas produced a disjointed public welfare program that was pushed and pulled between policies meant to enlarge the department and others intended to control its growth.

The debate over public relief spending and administration, however, affected the Overseers' two relief programs differently. After the passage of the Mothers' Aid program in 1913, the Overseers of the Poor began to divide relief cases into two categories, Mothers' Aid and Dependent Aid. Mothers' Aid provided financial support to poor mothers with dependent children. Dependent Aid was the "all other" category of relief, aiding the needy elderly, the intemperate, the unemployed, the sick and disabled, and poor mothers who could not qualify for Mothers' Aid. Between 1913 and 1919, Mothers' Aid accounted for most of the public welfare budget; however, after 1920, Dependent Aid grew to overshadow Mothers' Aid as expenditures on this program, particularly for unemployed families, surpassed the outlays for Mothers' Aid and pushed the Overseers' budget to unprecedented levels.[1]

While neither Irish nor Yankee politicians set Mothers' Aid against Dependent Aid, their competing views of the purpose of public assistance as well as their different attitudes toward women and gender roles created a poor relief program bifurcated between Mothers' Aid and Dependent Aid. Believing that the government should be willing to support a family so as to prevent potential breakdown, Boston's Irish politicians favored Dependent Aid, and they used this program to benefit unemployed male "breadwinners." Their demand for a larger and more generous relief program for "intact" families was at odds with the traditional notion of public aid as consolation after family breakdown caused by death, illness, old age, or desertion. Their focus on Dependent Aid, however, also reflected their discomfort with Mothers' Aid as a program aimed at women and overseen largely by female social workers.

In contrast, Yankee politicians agitated for administrative practices that would limit the use of welfare funds by "able-bodied" men and women. They also pressed for increased professional regulation and investigation of welfare recipients and pointed to the Mothers' Aid program as an example of a well-administered welfare program even if an expensive one. Their demand for welfare reform, however, had its greatest effect on Mothers' Aid, which during the twenties became increasingly regulated and supervised and which, as a result, saw a drop in its caseload and a limited increase in its budget as the twenties unfolded. Thus, local politics shaped and reshaped Boston's two public welfare programs, Mothers' Aid and Dependent Aid, and the Yankee politicians and social workers who insisted they wanted to remove public relief from politics were part of the politics.[2]

Social and Political Setting

The passage of the Mothers' Aid Act in 1913 and the implementation of that program through local public relief programs increased the political significance of the work of Overseers of the Poor. Like many other Progressive-era reforms, Mothers' Aid blurred the boundaries between the political and nonpolitical and brought governmental intervention into areas previously considered private. In Boston, this meant that over 1,500 poor mothers, most of whom had earlier relied on private charities or on their own meager resources, now looked to the Overseers of the Poor for support. With the introduction of Mothers' Aid, public poor relief in Boston increased more than 600 percent between 1912 and 1919. The increase was also affected by wartime inflation, but the unadjusted increase in public poor relief drove the political reaction. As Mothers' Aid swelled the Overseers' budget, municipal politicians began to focus on the city's relief program as they never had previously.[3]

But while the increased public expenditures on Mothers' Aid sparked political debate over relief, Boston's contentious social and political context fueled that debate. In Boston, as in other large U.S. cities, immigrants and second-generation immigrants had become the majority, and with that status came political opportunity. During the second half of the nineteenth century, the Irish became the dominant ethnic group in Boston. Initially, Irish politicians cooperated with the city's Yankee political leadership, but as ethnic tensions intensified with the swell of new immigration, the uneasy alliance broke down. The mayoral victory of a ward boss and outspoken critic of Boston's Yankee leadership, John F. Fitzgerald, over Yankee philanthropist James J. Storrow in 1909 marked the emergence of truly oppositional politics in Boston and the erosion of Yankee power. During the next twenty years, the Irish held a near monopoly in city government and were overrepresented in elective offices. The Irish did not create a political network, however, divided as they were by class and personality. As a result, no single "boss" wielded control; instead, ward leaders with personal followings competed with one another for political power, at times crafting alliances with other ethnic groups. Nevertheless, or perhaps as a consequence, the overarching political division in Boston became understood as one between immigrant stock and Yankee Bostonians.[4]

In response to a less accommodating political climate and the growing power of ethnic Democrats in the city, Yankee Republicans instigated city reform measures as a means of controlling immigrant political power and protecting Yankee interests. The consequence of city reform in Boston, however, only deepened ethnic antagonism and sharpened the division between Yankee and Irish politicians. Yankee business and political leaders pressured the Republican-controlled Massachusetts legislature to impose numerous restraints on city government. A 1909 city charter severely weakened the city's legislative branch, where Irish immigrants enjoyed their greatest power, and strengthened the authority of the mayor, an office the Republicans thought they could still control. For protection against too strong a mayor, especially an Irish one, the governor retained the power to appoint Boston's police commissioner and the city's licensing board; in addition, the legislature established the city's tax and debt limits. The new charter also made all city elections nonpartisan to weaken Democratic loyalties. Finally, the legislature established a Finance Commission, which became a powerful "watch-dog" agency with the power to subpoena witnesses and to launch investigations of city government. Although these reforms did not effectively curtail the Irish control of city government, they provided powerful tools to control municipal government and had a significant effect on welfare policy.[5]

The city's Irish politicians were not blind to the legislature's "control from without" and criticized the reforms. Claiming to speak for all immigrants, Boston's Irish leaders advanced a political agenda aimed at undermining the Yankee political establishment. They saw the major function of the government as providing its citizens safety and sanctuary, practical opportunities of social and economic advancement, and in time of need, the basic necessities of life. "I think that there's got to be in every ward somebody that any bloke can come to—no matter what he's done—and get help," ward boss Martin Lomasney reportedly said. "Help, you understand—none of your law and justice, but help." While evidence on Boston and other cities indicates that ward politicians were more talk than money and jobs, their rhetoric of enlarged governmental responsibility represented an ideological break from the traditional belief in limited governmental action and provision, a belief held dear by most of Boston's Yankees.[6]

Boston's most famous Irish mayor, James Michael Curley, embodied the oppositional politics of this era. Born into poverty, Curley's widowed mother had worked as a scrubwoman to support the family. An ambitious young man, Curley had used politics as a route away from the poverty of his childhood and as a step up from his own low-status jobs. He got his start in the ward politics of Roxbury, a working-class section of the city. He then became a member of the Common Council, an alderman, and then a city councilman in 1909. The next year, Curley won a seat in the U.S. House of Representatives, where he served two terms before returning to Boston to run for mayor in 1913. In and out of political office over the next four decades, he served as mayor from 1914 to 1918, 1922 to 1926, 1930 to 1934, and 1946 to 1950 and as governor from 1935 to 1937. Curley polarized immigrant and native-born interests as he agitated for an enlargement of government services, particularly for the less advantaged, immigrant populations. The city's Yankee leadership, as well as some ethnic leaders more firmly in the middle class, shuddered at Curley's approach to government, associating it with graft and corruption. Curley was, in fact, guilty of a fair amount of graft and petty corruption. Throughout his political career, he lived far beyond the level of his salary, most likely enjoying kickbacks from contractors given city business. In Boston as elsewhere, however, the amount of corruption associated with ethnic urban politics was limited and incommensurate to the outrage it generated among urban reformers.[7]

Ironically, the oppositional politics of Curley and others dovetailed with Progressive reforms, like the Mothers' Aid program, that also demanded enlarged governmental action and provision. In his first inaugural speech before the City Council, in 1914, Curley praised the city's increased spending on Mothers' Aid. Though he had played little role in the passage of this state program, he supported it: "Through this expenditure, poverty is robbed of its terrors, homes are preserved intact. Mothers are comforted with the companionship of their children, and children are reared under the watchful eye of their mother." He insisted that the program had ended "the long line of widows wending their way before sunrise and after the sun has set to office buildings . . . to eke out an existence for their children by the hardest character of manual labor, on their knees scrubbing." Curley called such labor by women "an indictment of our social system." To the program's critics, he asked: "Who is there in this or any other community so shortsighted and unmanly as to maintain that this expenditure is not justifiable?"[8]

By defending Mothers' Aid despite its increasing cost, Curley challenged members of the Yankee establishment in Boston who favored limited governmental expenses. Curley's experience as a son of a widow who had worked as a scrubwoman inspired his defense of the new program, as did his vision of government as a legitimate source of support for the needy. However, by casting his vision of social provisions in terms of governmental "duty" and by castigating the opponents of Mothers' Aid as "unmanly," Curley departed from the maternalistic arguments that infused the campaign for Mothers' Aid and put a distinctly masculine spin on the welfare debate. Curley saw Mothers' Aid more in terms of "support" for poor families who had suffered from an unjust social and economic system rather than as necessarily a "caring" program administered by and for women. As the welfare debate unfolded in the 1920s, these competing ideas about the purpose of welfare would come into conflict.

Demands for Enlargement

Curley's support for the Mothers' Aid program marked the beginning of the political debate over public aid in Boston. Irish politicians, along with Curley, took the offensive in this debate, agitating for a larger and more democratically responsive public welfare program. The dominance of Irish politicians was, in part, a reflection of their majority control of elected municipal positions, but it was also a consequence of the persistently low economic achievement of the Irish in Boston. Irish politicians were more vocal about welfare policies because more of them had experienced poverty themselves and because many of their Irish constituents were clustered in the lower economic strata, if not in outright poverty. The Irish population's longer tenure in Boston and growing access to local political power during the second half of the nineteenth century had raised expectations and opened opportunities to some of the city's Irish, but most experienced only limited economic advancement. As late as the turn of the century, more than half of Irish men in Boston worked as laborers, and few of them earned a living wage.[9]

There was some political self-interest, not to mention arrogance, in assuming the mantle for all immigrant groups. But these Irish politicians based their claim to speak for all poor Bostonians on their own familiarity with poverty and on a humanitarian desire to defend and to aid other poor groups. Curley called himself the "mayor of the poor," not just the Irish poor. Likewise, the Irish on the City Council insisted that their pleas for enlarged welfare spending would benefit all their poor constituents. "Poverty is no disgrace," announced Councilman Jerry Watson, admitting that he had lived in poverty as a young boy. "I made up my mind then—it got into my bones— that I would try to do what I could for the ordinary man or woman who needed help." "Ordinary" people of whatever ethnic background became the rallying point for these Irish politicians.[10]

Boston's other major immigrant groups, Italians and Jews, had mixed reactions to the presumption of the Irish to speak for all poor immigrant groups. During the first two decades of the twentieth century, Boston's Italians had little political power of their own, and they supported Irish Democrats. In contrast, Boston's Jewish population represented a larger economic spectrum and had become politically active, often in concert with the city's Republican leaders. Unlike Boston's Italians, Jewish voters in Dorchester (Ward 14) managed to elect one of their own to the City Council. The Jewish representatives on the City Council often resisted their Irish colleagues' attempts to position themselves as spokesmen for all poor immigrants. There is no evidence, however, that they fought the efforts of Irish politicians to enlarge public welfare programs.[11]

As part of their effort to bring government to the "ordinary" person, Boston's Irish politicians recast public aid as a necessary and justified city expense. To Curley and Irish members of the City Council, the best way to serve the poor was to increase expenditures on public welfare, and, during the 1920s they annually increased the municipal relief budget. When these increases required the city to borrow against future revenue—something the Yankee leadership found abhorrent—the Irish politicians maintained: "When we are going to take care of the destitute of our city we should not quibble over whether it is good finance or bad finance." Breaking with the Yankee Republican's balanced-budget philosophy, the Irish members of the City Council were early believers in deficit spending, especially if it meant immediate relief to the city's poor and reassured the support of their constituents. In annual speeches before the City Council, Curley demanded a "generous policy" toward the poor. He argued that it was "the primary duty of the city to provide for its dependents." During his first administration (1914–18), his rhetoric was more pronounced than his fiscal support for the Overseers, a group he early on considered part of the Yankee establishment that he detested. As he began making his own appointments to the board, however, he gained more confidence in the Overseers' work. Later in his first term and consistently during his second term (1922–26), he submitted the full request from the department to the City Council for its approval, and he appropriated money for construction of a new public welfare building to replace the dilapidated headquarters built in 1869. A larger public assistance program—both in terms of budget and visibility—was part of Curley's effort to redefine governmental responsibility for the poor.[12]

Following this tack, the city's Irish politicians depicted reductions in public welfare expenditures as synonymous with mistreating the poor. The two Yankee mayors elected during this period, Andrew J. Peters (1918–22) and Malcolm E. Nichols (1926–30), faced severe criticism when they tried to curb the rising costs of poor aid. Members of the City Council accused Mayor Nichols of "build[ing] up his own political fences on the needs of the poor people of the City of Boston" when he refused to fund the public aid program. The *Evening Transcript*, the paper of Yankee Bostonians, defended the mayor, but the *Post*, the paper of working-class Democrats, spotlighted the critics of Nichols's welfare cuts in an article titled "Huge Cuts in City Relief Denounced." Curley, who spent his time out of office campaigning for the next election, got into the act, calling it "an outrage to cut the allowances to the poor of the city." Nichols had assumed a broader support for his fiscal conservatism, and the outcry took him by surprise. He quickly shifted blame onto the Board of Overseers and requested that they restore the amount cut from each relief case. The board resented Nichols's attempt to pass the blame, and several members criticized him. In response, Nichols fired three members of the board, including the respected Jewish chairman, Simon Hecht. His action against Hecht seriously jeopardized Nichols's support in the Jewish community and among the leaders of Boston's private Jewish welfare organizations. Cutting relief payments had become a political liability.[13]

In their defense of public assistance, Irish politicians often personalized the plight of their poor constituents, casting a positive light on the efforts of the poor in the face of poverty. The politicians told stories of old men and women, struggling families with children, and widowed mothers. All of these they called the "poor unfortunates." These examples, some rhetorical and some, no doubt, based on real cases, proved powerful in promoting belief in enlarged governmental responsibility for the poor. In speeches and in debates in the City Council, the politicians portrayed the poor as victims of circumstances beyond their control. The councilmen shifted the burden of morality from the victim of poverty to the government, demanding that the political system demonstrate its own morality in caring for the poor rather than asking the poor to prove their moral worth. Their depiction of the poor and their demand for governmental action were a distinct departure from the nineteenth-century equation of poverty with individual moral failing. Likewise, their insistence that the government assume responsibility for the needy was also a break from the laissez-faire philosophy of the earlier period.

Their views about poverty and governmental responsibility led them to broaden their demands for public aid to include and even give preference to families of unemployed men. Over the course of the decade, they frequently integrated images of poor families headed by unemployed breadwinners into the political debate. One councilman described a poor family that was getting the runaround by public and private welfare programs. Another described letters from "men with families, with five, six or seven children, who have appealed to the Overseers and could only get a grocery order." Another recounted his effort for "worthy cases," which he identified as men with wives and children: "There is no politics with me in these matters, none of the 'good fellow' business. I know them. Unless they are married I don't go there [to the Overseers to advocate their case], because I believe that only the meritorious cases should be helped." Even Curley, who during the teens had relied on the images of poor widowhood to justify increased welfare outlays, more often mentioned the needs of the unemployed when submitting appropriations for public aid during his second administration, in the twenties.[14]

The increased emphasis on the needs of unemployed men with families reflected the high unemployment in Boston in the early twenties, but it also was part of an effort by city councilmen to legitimatize the use of poor relief for the unemployed. These politicians argued that a married couple with children was "meritorious" and "worthy" of public aid in the face of economic hardship. While Protestant charity officials and the Overseers criticized large families, these Irish politicians saw them as only more reason for the need for governmental support. Moreover, they argued that governmental support should come before family emergencies struck. If a work requirement was attached to the aid provided the unemployed, the councilmen argued, the pay should equal a fair wage. In their demands they referred to the public welfare disbursement as "a week's pay," and complained that the department did not adequately provide "poor unfortunates enough to live on, parents and children." In their arguments and in their descriptions of the needy, they attempted to establish public aid as a legitimate source of support for families with unemployed male wage earners, ending the traditional view of public aid as reserved for only those destitute and without families.[15]

In demanding aid for the unemployed that was adequate and without stigma, the councilmen echoed the earlier campaign for Mothers' Aid. Using the language of the Mothers' Aid movement, they argued that poor families "deserved" governmental support in time of need. Like the earlier campaign for widows' aid, their argument for more generous relief payments stressed the family responsibilities of the poor, but the city councilmen focused on the role of fathers and not mothers in providing family support. Unlike the Mothers' Aid advocates, these city councilmen did not attach a "fitness" measure to their proposals. While a woman's "worthiness" for Mothers' Aid was related to individual "moral" behavior, no similar measure was attached to the unemployment relief proposed by these city councilmen. "Worthiness" for unemployment relief was assumed, given a man's status as a breadwinner.

In their political offensive, Boston's Irish politicians also addressed the administration of public aid in Boston. Curley and other Irish politicians complained, sometimes bitterly, about the treatment of the poor by the Overseers and demanded that the members and staff of the Overseers become more politically accountable for their actions. As Councilman John I. Fitzgerald put it, "These overseers ought to be brought to time and told a thing or two." During this period, the City Council passed orders that the Overseers show more respect for the poor and denounced what they called "a high handed attitude" on the part of social workers in the department. They accused the visitors of acting as if the money dispensed was theirs and not the city's, and they criticized the amount of investigation conducted by the department. Councilman John F. Dowd, for example, reported that a visitor from the welfare department had badgered a family in his district beginning with an inspection of the breakfast early in the morning and ending with a visit by the social worker at ten o'clock at night. He alleged that the social worker accused the family of "'living rather high.'" Dowd protested: "We want people to carry out the law, but we don't want detectives on the pay roll of the Department of Public Welfare." Using more sentimental language, Mayor Curley supported the effort of the members of the City Council, saying that he, too, had "long cherished the hope that a little more of human kindness might enter into our treatment of the unfortunate poor."[16]

Curley and many Irish members of the City Council, including several not aligned with Curley, saw their defense of public aid recipients as part of the democratic process. They believed that as elected officials they should have direct oversight of the public aid department. In describing their attempts to intervene for welfare recipients, these politicians brought specific cases to the public's attention, and some even asked that the department provide them with a list of welfare recipients in their wards. The opponents of their approach to welfare policy—primarily Republicans on the City Council and Yankee social workers—accused them of political corruption and fraud. The opponents resisted the discussion of specific cases within the political debate, claiming to protect public aid recipients from embarrassment. Nevertheless, the critics of the welfare department continued to bring specific cases to the debate, an approach that violated the long-standing practice of reserving discretion for the Overseers.[17]

The antagonism of Curley and the City Council toward the Overseers was in response to the continued dominance of Anglo-Saxons on the board and staff of the welfare department. Even though the board had a Jewish member and, occasionally, an Irish member, the majority of the Overseers were "outstanding citizens" whose families had long resided in the city and whose political ties were with the Yankee Republican political leadership. Beginning in his first administration, Curley made appointments to the board from a different pool of "outstanding citizens," appointing Irish and Italians in large enough numbers to assure the selection of Walter V. McCarthy to run the daily operations of the department. He was the first Catholic to hold this position.[18]

Nevertheless, civil service requirements mandating professional credentials in social work slowed the ethnic integration of the Overseers board and staff. Members of the City Council recognized this and bitterly criticized it. "Under the so-called social service's regime," complained Councilman Dowd, "they have schools conducted by high-toned reformers who must find positions for those who are turned out, and positions are promised through civil service regulations." Advocates of social work education described professionalization in terms of efficiency and modernization, but most of Boston's Irish politicians saw it as a means for Yankee Bostonians to maintain their control over public aid in Boston.[19]

The councilmen did not limit their attacks to the Overseers but also criticized the large nonsectarian charities and their Protestant leaders. The Associated Charities, renamed the Family Welfare Society (FWS) in 1920, came under particular attack. "Why, I cannot figure here the name of an immigrant or the son of an immigrant in the whole outfit," Councilman Jerry Watson complained about the FWS. He then told about the experience of one of his constituents with the FWS: "A short time ago a family out my way were in need. They got in touch with a visitor from the Overseers of the Poor, and instead of getting the help they expected, they were advised to see a representative of the FWS. A visitor from the organization came to see them, and the woman very foolishly told the visitor that if she could not be helped she would see Jerry Watson. She was told, 'Politicians don't bother us. You know, Mrs. So and So, that no Catholic contributes to FWS the fund.'" To members of the City Council like Watson, the FWS failed to appreciate the unofficial welfare services of the ward leaders. These politicians resented the informal coordination between the Overseers and FWS, particularly since the FWS often took a strong stand against direct relief to the poor. The FWS, in their opinion, did not deserve a place in the Charity Building. "We are harboring in a city building an organization [FWS] made up of practical professional philanthropists, who feed the starving on kind words and smiles," Councilman Watson declared in 1922. "Why, it is a disgrace to the city to permit them to occupy one foot of our property. The idea of contaminating the St. Vincent de Paul Society, the Jewish Welfare Society and all other relief organizations by permitting these proselytizing propagandists, begging philanthropists to conduct [business in the same building]!"[20]

In their demands for a more democratically controlled welfare department and in their attack on the Overseers and organizations like the FWS, Curley and members of the City Council displayed particular antagonism toward female social workers. The FWS visitors who came under attack were well-known to be women. Though the public welfare department employed more male than female visitors, the councilmen concentrated on tales of oppressive investigation by female visitors. The "social service's regime," according to Councilman Dowd, had produced a "meddlesome gang . . . [who] go around to the home and do things that are absolutely unwarranted." This "meddlesome gang" was connected with the new program in social work at Simmons College, a women's college in Boston. In an attack a few years later on the Social Service Exchange, the index used to track families receiving public and private aid, the council singled out the female director of the Exchange. Called "Miss Peggy Pry" on the floor of the City Council, Margaret Woodside was accused of having too much power over the recipients of public aid. Foreshadowing sentiments of the 1930s, members of the City Council demanded that the welfare department dismiss married female employees, whose employment there contradicted what these politicians considered an important mission of the department, supporting unemployed men. Curley echoed their sentiments in his appointments to the Board of Overseers, naming far fewer women to the board than either earlier or contemporary Yankee administrations.[21]

The criticism of female social workers illuminates the nature of the welfare debate during this period. The professionalization of these women challenged these politicians' notions of women's proper place in society. When the politicians demanded that the staff be "told a thing or two," and when they created an image of a domineering female social worker, they were expressing contempt for the power that women social workers were gaining through professional activity and the feminism that undergirded much of these women's professional aspirations. Class and ethnic strife fueled the criticism since most of the graduates of the new training schools at this time were, in fact, middle-class and Anglo-Saxon. The politicians' most bitter comments, however, were aimed at these social workers as women. The criticism was part of the conservative backlash against women in the 1920s, but it was also a critique of the "maternal" model of welfare popular among Protestant charity leaders and social reformers. Arguments about women's proclivity for social work or about poor women's need for supervision were absent from the city councilmen's discussion of welfare. If anything, these politicians, few of whom were far removed economically from the poor, wanted social work purged of watchfulness and control. With their criticism of women and women's social work, they implicitly attacked the Mothers' Aid program, which, unlike the Dependent Aid program, was framed along maternal lines—that is, closely supervised, aimed at women, and directed by female social workers. The appointment of Elizabeth Moloney, an Irish Catholic, to run Mothers' Aid at the state level did not dissuade the critics from associating the program with the native-born charity officials who initially implemented the program.

Even as Curley and members of the City Council generated a substantial political debate over public aid, they never achieved a united front in their demand for an enlarged public welfare program. Unlike other cities, Boston never saw the development of a political machine, nor did it ever have a "boss" politician. Though a powerful leader, Curley never created an extensive political network through which to exert influence, and he had little sway with the small but growing number of middle-class Irish who sought to distance themselves from Curley's antagonistic approach and reputation for corruption. As a result, Curley was never assured the full support of the City Council, and its members never completely trusted him. Moreover, since the state legislature controlled the municipal tax rate and the debt level, Curley's power to enlarge the municipal budget was limited. Nevertheless, speaking for the "ordinary" men and women of Boston, Curley and members of the City Council brought the policies and practices of the Overseers of the Poor into the contentious political debate that divided Boston at this time.

Defensive Response

As Irish politicians pushed to enlarge welfare expenditures and to require more political accountability from the Overseers, Yankee politicians, together with social work professionals, tried to limit the growth of public aid in Boston. Boston's Yankee establishment was outraged by the increasing welfare expenditures, opposing any growth of governmental functions because of the tax consequences. But the establishment was also offended by the Irish politicians' attempt to enlarge governmental responsibility because it weakened the control that Yankee Bostonians had exerted over poor relief. Yankee political leaders tried both to curb and to control the expansion of public welfare, and their efforts, like the efforts of the Irish politicians, affected the programs for poor relief in Boston during the 1920s.

The administrations of the two Yankee mayors during this period give the clearest indication of the opposition of Yankee Boston to the enlargement of governmental responsibility advocated by Curley and Irish politicians on the City Council. Advancing ideas of municipal efficiency and fiscal restraint, Andrew Peters, a Yankee Democrat, defeated Curley in 1917. He began attacking the increased expenditures by the Overseers almost immediately after taking office. He refused to request additional funding for the department until the Overseers cut their caseload and, even then, cut their request by $5,000 before sending it to the City Council for approval. When his fiscal policy proved only marginally effective, Peters blamed the state-mandated Mothers' Aid requirements for the continued increases. During subsequent years of his term, when expenditures on both Dependent Aid and Mothers' Aid climbed, Peters blamed the postwar recession. His inability to control the growing city budget and his half-hearted support of public welfare expenditures won him few supporters from either end of the political spectrum. Curley capitalized on Peters's unpopularity, defeating him in 1921 by campaigning as the "people's" mayor and by promising an administration more responsive to the needs of poor citizens.[22]

When Curley was prevented from succeeding himself, Yankee Republican Malcolm Nichols became the mayor in 1926, and increasing welfare expenditures again became a topic of concern. A former state legislator and a Harding-appointed internal revenue collector in Boston, Nichols enjoyed the support of Republicans and the endorsement of the Good Government Association, a Progressive reform organization that had ties to the city's business community. As mayor, he took a decidedly different approach to city spending than Curley had, stressing economy and not government largess. "No municipal budget should be increased without thought about the ways and means of payment," he asserted in his inaugural speech. He continued: "This old and respectable principle is sometimes lost in the lure of wishing for things. We all like more and more parks, playgrounds, concerts, celebrations, buildings, and other attractive municipal services, and we shall have them too, in reason I hope, always bearing in mind that their cost is reflected in the tax rate." Nichols targeted the municipal projects Curley had initiated, including public welfare. Nichols doubted that the enlarged public welfare budget reflected an increase of poverty in the city. Rather, he suspected that private charities were transferring cases to the public department to lighten their own financial burden and that public relief had become tainted by political corruption. Nichols's reading of public welfare expansion represented the position of most fiscal conservatives, who believed that the needs of the poor should be met primarily through private charities and who feared that a large public welfare program would lead to excessive, and even fraudulent, claims.[23]

Throughout his term, Nichols tried to limit the growth of public aid programs. He cut the budget requests of the Overseers and contended that, through better administration and more rigorous investigation of cases, the department would be able to support the "truly needy" despite budget reductions. He implied that under Curley's administration some recipients of public aid had not been "truly" in need. He reduced the borrowing orders approved during the Curley administration for construction of the public welfare building and opened the new building in March 1925 with little fanfare. To assure the implementation of his fiscal policy, Nichols appointed members to the Board of Overseers who shared his outlook: two social workers, Nina M. Gevalt and Eva Whiting White, and a close friend, George H. Johnson, who was also the city collector. The following year, Nichols took an even stronger step toward controlling the Overseers when he fired four board members who had been appointed by previous mayors; those fired included Simon E. Hecht, the respected Jewish chairman. A wealthy wool merchant, Hecht had originally been appointed to the Overseers by a Republican mayor in 1908, and he was not aligned with Curley's populist political agenda. However, Nichols fired him for publicly criticizing the cuts in welfare funding the mayor had favored. Open discussion of welfare policy, a product of the antagonistic political climate in Boston, was something Nichols was intent on bringing to a close.[24]

The fierce criticism Nichols faced for his attempts to reduce public aid and to purge the Board of Overseers limited his ability to make across-the-board cuts in expenditures. As a result, overall expenditures on poor relief continued to increase during his administration just as they had during Peters's administration. Insufficient appropriations simply forced the Overseers to request additional funding before the end of the year. These additional funds—requested close to Christmas—easily passed the City Council. Nichols's demands for fiscal constraint did lead, however, to a reduction in Mothers' Aid expenditures. While never directly attacking the program, he appropriated less funding for it. He also supported administrative reforms of the welfare department, and these reforms had a greater effect on the Mothers' Aid program than on overall expenditures or administration. The disproportional effect of these reforms on the Mothers' Aid program is ironic since both the Yankee political leadership and professional social workers considered it the "better run" welfare program in comparison with general poor relief.[25]

Advanced by the city's business leadership and social work professionals, the welfare reform movement aimed to reduce overall costs of public relief through increased regulation and more extensive investigation of public aid cases. Despite the additional costs associated with these types of reform, the advocates of these reforms argued that they would reduce welfare expenditures in the long run. Yankee politicians, like Nichols, supported tighter administrative control over welfare and the promise of fiscal constraint, and they pressed for administrative reforms at the Overseers. They did not, however, advance their case on the floor of the Irish-controlled City Council. Instead, they worked through the Finance Commission (FinCom). A product of the Charter Reform of 1909, the Finance Commission was a watchdog committee appointed by the governor. During the teens and twenties, Yankee Republicans dominate the FinCom much as they dominated state politics, and they saw their main goal as uncovering corruption among the city's Irish Democratic politicians. The rapid increases in public aid expenditures and the strong Irish political support for these increases prompted the FinCom to investigate the department numerous times during this period. They relied on leaders of the major Protestant charities as well as on professional social workers to conduct these investigations.[26]

The Finance Commission's reports during the twenties reflected the blend of consternation and resignation that the Yankee political leaders felt about the enlarging public relief expenditures of the period. No doubt to the disappointment of fiscal conservatives like mayors Peters and Nichols, the FinCom did not find much misconduct in the department. It traced the increases in public aid to the concept of "adequate support" introduced by the Mothers' Aid Act and to the weakening of the residency requirements. In addition, the FinCom noted "a change in the attitude toward the stigma of receiving aid from the poor department," meaning a weakening of the popular sentiment against the use of public aid. The commission concluded that legislative initiatives as well as new ideas about the acceptability of public dependency would make cutting welfare programs impossible, and it recommended instead improved administration of poor relief as a means of curtailing expenses.[27]

The FinCom's idea of improved administration differed considerably from the position of the Irish councilmen, who were, likewise, agitating for changes in the department's administration. While the critics of the Overseers on the City Council demanded less scrutiny of public aid recipients, the FinCom demanded more. "Careful supervision and study of cases" would be possible through the hiring of additional "trained" visitors, according to the reports. Since professionalization would entail casework, it was thought that fraudulent cases would be purged from the welfare rolls. Thus, professionalization would be a means of curbing welfare expenditures. However, the FinCom also believed professionalization would limit political accountability. Standards set by professional organizations would substitute for measures of political accountability. The department's staff would not be expected to answer to politicians, particularly those on the City Council.

The FinCom did not display the antagonism toward female social workers that pervaded the criticism of public welfare by City Council members; in fact, the FinCom relied on female social workers to conduct its investigations and consistently recommended that the department hire additional female visitors. The female visitors employed by the state to supervise Mothers' Aid cases, the FinCom argued, had proved to be particularly effective in closely supervising their cases. Moreover, their relatively low salaries would ensure that the cost of their positions would not exceed the savings that their investigative work would produce. For the FinCom, professionalization became synonymous with hiring more women social workers whose casework method would more closely regulate the distribution of poor relief. While the commission did not employ the term "maternalism," it recommended a system in which women aided and supervised poor women.[28]

As the twenties progressed, the Overseers adopted many of the recommendations of the FinCom. The size of the staff increased with the hiring of more professional social workers, including a number of women visitors. However, the policy of increased scrutiny of aid cases was applied more rigorously to Mothers' Aid cases than to Dependent Aid cases. The newly "trained" women visitors were assigned primarily to Mothers' Aid cases, and those cases were supervised closely. The additional supervision reduced the number of cases both by eliminating unqualified cases and by discouraging enrollment through bureaucratic harassment. The FinCom noted the difference between the administration of Mothers' Aid and Dependent Aid. It criticized the Dependent Aid program for dispensing relief with only "a perfunctory investigation" and without "any definite plan," while it saluted the quarterly visits required by the Mothers' Aid legislation. The FinCom believed that regular visits would assure an ongoing investigation of Mothers' Aid recipients and rapid implementation of "the plan," meaning finding a way to close the cases as soon as possible.

The administrative policies advocated by the Finance Commission proved powerful in shaping the public aid program in Boston. The investigation and supervision of relief recipients became the stated goal of the welfare department, even if the goal was most consistently applied to the Mothers' Aid program. The employment of female social workers to conduct the supervision became routine. The professional expertise of these specially trained social workers, the FinCom conjectured, justified their actions and removed them from political accountability. The aim of these reforms was to dilute—if not to end—the influence of Boston's Irish politicians on the politics of public aid; however, the consequence was a bifurcation of public aid. The product of ethnic conflict more than a vision for adequate care for the poor, Boston's welfare policy was simultaneously constrained and enlarged during the 1920s.

Changes in Public Aid

The political debate over poor relief fundamentally changed the scope and shape of public aid in Boston during the 1920s. The amount of public aid distributed directly to the poor nearly tripled with steady annual increases. Adjusted for the cost of living, which showed a sharp drop between 1920 and 1921 and then remained fairly constant, expenditures more than tripled. The additional spending on poor relief far outstripped increases in expenditures by the city as a whole. The rising costs of public aid were driven, in part, by the larger caseload. More than doubling, the department's total caseload rose from 3,605 in 1920 to 7,463 in 1929. The enlarged expenditures, however, also reflected an increased average grant per case, an amount that rose 36 percent in unadjusted figures and 54 percent adjusted for the cost of living.[29]

The Dependent Aid program was the site of most of the growth of the public welfare program during the 1920s. As the "all other" relief program, the Dependent Aid caseload included the elderly, the unemployed, the sick and disabled, and mothers who could not qualify for Mothers' Aid. Traditionally, the majority of Dependent Aid cases were elderly women with no family to support them, but during the 1920s, the Dependent Aid program aided a larger number of the city's unemployed than it had previously. These new welfare recipients were largely men out of work with families to support.[30]

Between 1920 and 1929, expenditures on Dependent Aid grew more than sevenfold, rising from $138,728 to $1,046,770. Adjusted for cost-of-living changes, this represented an even greater increase in real dollars. Just as the growth in Dependent Aid funding was greater than the increase in total expenditures, the enlargement in the Dependent Aid caseload surpassed the increase in aggregate caseload. The Dependent Aid caseload tripled, from 1,978 in 1920 to 6,347 in 1929. Average grant per case for Dependent Aid also more than doubled as the "adequate income" stipulation of the Mothers' Aid program became the measure, in theory at least, of support to families with unemployed male wage earners. In contrast, Mothers' Aid showed little expansion during the twenties, especially compared with Dependent Aid. Between 1913 and 1924, the Mothers' Aid program had represented the larger share of the city's public aid expenditures and showed yearly increases in expenditures. Beginning in 1922, however, its expenditures leveled off, and in some years decreased. Over the course of the decade, the program's expenditures rose only 13 percent. The Mothers' Aid caseload was also constrained, falling 1,544 to 975 between 1920 and 1929, a 37 percent drop.[31]

Taken together, the increases in total expenditures, caseload, and grant size indicate that the city of Boston was assuming greater responsibility for providing for the poor. Moreover, the increased caseload indicates that a larger proportion of the city's population was using public aid, suggesting that public support was becoming less shameful or stigmatized. However, the difference between Dependent Aid and Mothers' Aid suggests that the needs of the city's unemployed were driving the increases in public aid during the twenties. Thus, although Mothers' Aid had initiated the expansion of public aid in the 1910s, Dependent Aid, specifically aid to unemployed men, eclipsed public aid for poor women with children in the 1920s.

Debated and shaped within the contentious political arena of the 1920s, Boston's public welfare program was transformed. By the end of the twenties, Irish politicians had succeeded in assuring that the city spent a significantly larger amount of its budget on poor relief. In discussing welfare expenditures and welfare policy on the floor of the City Council, they brought the operations of the Overseers of the Poor into the democratic arena for the first time. The ensuing political dispute over welfare was not simply over fiscal expansion or constraint; embedded within the debate were also conflicting ideas about the purpose and model of relief operations, the consequence of which was an increasing differentiation between Mothers' Aid and Dependent Aid. The political debate over welfare and the disjointed expansion of Boston's public welfare expenditures set the stage for the policy struggles of the next decade. With the crisis of the Depression, the debate would continue, new issues would unfold, and new political alliances would be crafted.

4 PRIVATE CHARITIES, 1920–1929

T HE ENLARGEMENT of public welfare that sent shock waves through Boston politics reverberated among the city's private charities as well. With the introduction of Mothers' Aid in 1913 and the enlargement of Dependent Aid during the twenties, public assistance became available to a larger number of the city's poor, many of whom had previously relied on private charity. As a result, the city's private charities began to move away from their own relief operations and recast their programs as "family welfare." This process began the restructuring of poor relief as primarily a public function and pushed private charities in the direction of social services. In some ways, the expanding role of the public poor relief program diminished differences among the city's private charities as they began to define themselves, not against one another, but in contrast to the city's public welfare operations. In more important ways, however, significant differences persisted among the city's Catholic, Jewish, and Protestant charities, as they renegotiated their positions in relation to an expanded public welfare program. During the 1920s, Boston's private charities responded differently to the enlargement of public relief operations, and they took different steps as they moved away from relief and toward family services. Moreover, they held different views on the family and on gender relations within families as well as different ideas about the types of services that families needed.[1]

The varied responses of Boston's private charities to the enlargement of public welfare in the 1920s suggest that the realignment of public and private welfare was more complex than the standard interpretations have suggested. First, while the emerging professionalization of social work affected the realignment of public and private welfare, its effects were uneven on the local level. Throughout the 1920s, private charities remained under the direction of men and women with no formal training in social work, and the practices associated with this new field, specifically casework and psychiatric methodology, were not applied uniformly. Largely an academic development, professional social work did not have a significant impact on the daily functioning of charities during the 1920s. Second, the dominance of the Protestant charities network, while powerful, was not total. As during the campaign for widows' pensions, Protestant charity leaders struggled during the 1920s to determine the shape of public and private welfare, and they used the language and practices of professional social work as a means to ensure their dominance. However, even more than during the campaign for widows' pensions, Boston's Catholic and Jewish charities, like their Protestant counterparts, influenced welfare policy that shaped the emerging public welfare program. Third, and perhaps most important, while the arena of family service created a potential site of consensus among private charities during the 1920s, the private charities did not share the same vision of gender relations within the family.[2]

Like the enlargement of public welfare, the realignment of public and private welfare in the 1920s evolved in the context of the increasing social and political influence of Boston's immigrant and immigrant-stock populations and the waning power of the city's Yankee Republicans. The negotiation between and among private charities during this time contributed to the trend toward increased public responsibility for cash assistance to the poor and established new relationships among private charities. The persistent differences among private charities and their various and shifting relations to the public welfare program, however, complicated the realignment of public and private responsibilities, not just retarding the development of public welfare in general, but also ensuring fragmentation and inconsistency among the city's relief programs.

Private Charities: Protestant, Catholic, and Jewish

During the 1920s, Boston's Protestant charities remained critical of the enlargement of public welfare and sought to control it. They had opposed the proposed widows' subsidies program and had drafted alternative legislation for a Mothers' Aid program that they believed would limit enrollment and contain costs. Despite their efforts, the Mothers' Aid program in Boston enrolled far more families than had previously received public aid. The increased public aid budget prompted the leaders of the Boston Provident Association and the Associated Charities, now named the Family Welfare Society, to accuse the Mothers' Aid program of fostering increased "dependency" on public aid—something these leaders considered detrimental to both taxpayers and the program's recipients.[3]

When the politics and economics of the 1920s began pressing for enlarged relief expenditures beyond the Mothers' Aid program, the Protestant charity leaders intensified their opposition to an expanded public welfare program. Although they conceded that the high unemployment of 1921 required governmental action, they insisted that assistance be temporary and limited. Long-term assistance to the unemployed, they argued, would foster laziness and dependency—the same argument they had made in opposition to the widows' pension campaign. Stressing what they believed was the need for personal accountability, the Protestant charity leaders saw the economic difficulties of the unemployed as largely their own doing. "The unemployed group," reported the BPA in 1923, "consists of those who are apt to be less efficient—the first to be discharged, the last to be employed. . . . Their shortcomings are sometimes due to a mental twist or physical difficulty, sometimes to a lack of training in any special line." Public relief, according to the BPA and the FWS, was not "discerning" enough to deal with the "individual" problems of the unemployed. Moreover, they argued that long-term aid to the unemployed would be costly, and they pointed to recent increases in public welfare expenditures as evidence. Defending their position, they contended that assistance to the unemployed was "abnormal."[4]

The Protestant charity leadership also opposed proposals for an old age pension in the state. Whether rich or poor, all individuals, they argued, should be responsible for saving for old age. If they could not, then family members should care for them. An old age pension would both discourage "thrift" and unduly tax society for what, these Protestant charity leaders believed, was a family responsibility. Throughout the 1910s and 1920s, they lobbied against proposals for old age pensions in Massachusetts. When popular support for an old age pension mounted in the late 1920s, they derailed the effort by proposing an Old Age Assistance program that, like Mothers' Aid, would include a means test and would be administered by the Overseers of the Poor. Their proposed measure became law in 1930.[5]

Boston's Protestant charity leaders conceded that, as the FWS's 1922 report put it, "there [was] a tendency to look more than formerly to public relief." But the leaders opposed the increased use of public relief by people not traditionally public aid recipients, namely the unemployed and elderly with families. This "tendency," they begrudgingly reported, reflected the "greater satisfaction of beneficiaries from a form of aid which many persons

consider to be their right." Public aid, they believed, should remain a prerogative of the Overseers, not an entitlement based on notions of social
rights. More important than philosophy, though, to these fiscally conservative charity leaders was the increased taxation associated with this "new tendency." They wanted the expansion of public welfare contained to limit the
city's budget and its tax rate.[6]

The Protestant charity leaders warned of the "dangers" of public welfare
expansion, namely an increased use of public welfare programs by the poor
and the consequential increase in taxes. But this danger could be limited,
they argued, if public welfare recipients were more regulated and supervised. The leaders of the BPA and the FWS pointed to the Mothers' Aid program as a "good" public aid program, particularly after the expenditures
on Mothers' Aid leveled off in the mid-twenties and enrollment dropped.
They saw the close supervision of Mothers' Aid clients and the program's
rigorous eligibility requirements as fulfilling what they considered "modern" social work practice, and they boasted about their involvement in the
drafting of Mothers' Aid. Noting the new practices of the Mothers' Aid program, the FWS, long critical of the relief efforts of the Overseers, wrote that
"those public officials . . . are doing their duty better than formerly," because
like private charities, public welfare was beginning to "individualize" its
work.[7]

Thus, even as they argued against the growth of public welfare, Boston's
Protestant charity leaders began to express a guarded acceptance of some
forms of public aid and to participate in discussions about public welfare reform during the 1920s. Working with the city's Finance Commission and
with the Nichols administration, they drafted recommendations for the hiring of additional caseworkers to investigate more thoroughly the needs of
applicants and to supervise better their use of public funds.[8]

As part of these reforms, the Protestant charity leaders suggested that
private agencies, particularly the ones they represented, act as consultants on
public welfare. Thereby, private aid organizations would monitor public
welfare departments closely to prevent waste and corruption. As consultants, private agencies could experiment with welfare initiatives that might
later become public programs. The Protestant charity leaders also envisioned using the Council of Social Agencies, an association of private charities, to influence public welfare policy and administration.

By suggesting that private charities act as consultants, the city's Protestant
charity leaders were attempting to protect the informal interchange between

Boston's public relief department and the Protestant charities that had existed since before the expansion of the Overseers program and the political changes in the city. During the 1920s, however, they recast this interaction as a feature of "modern" social work. William H. Pear, general agent of the BPA, urged the city's public and private welfare operations to take unified action against poverty and need. He contended that Boston was already providing a good example of "effective interaction" among private agencies, cooperation between public and private relief, and cutting-edge casework methodology. He cited Mothers' Aid case studies as examples of his interpretation. For example, he described a "Mrs. Macbeth" who was receiving $20 a week from Mothers' Aid but who also relied on health services and social services from private agencies. A visitor from the BPA, Pear explained, coordinated Mrs. Macbeth's aid in cooperation with the visitor from the Overseers. He argued that this type of coordination assured professional standards of care while limiting public costs.[9]

Even as Protestant charity leaders, like Pear, struggled to maintain their influence within the city's relief system, they were losing ground. Despite their claims of mutual public and private cooperation, the implementation of Mothers' Aid and the expansion of Dependent Aid during the 1920s represented a threat to the power of these private organizations. Former clients of the FWS and BPA began to turn to the public welfare department, particularly those who could qualify for the higher-paying Mothers' Aid program. Moreover, as the "adequate support" clause of Mothers' Aid increased the level of aid, public welfare recipients were less likely to need to patch together assistance from numerous charities. The BPA and the AC had long acted as referral services for families as they made this effort, but with public aid levels increasing, the private charities' role as charity brokers was increasingly unnecessary.[10]

The BPA and the FWS were also facing financial difficulties during the 1920s. During the war, both organizations had run deficits, as subscriptions and investment income fell while demands for services increased. Moreover, their administrative costs were increasing as they began hiring more salaried social workers. Faced with these economic difficulties, the BPA and FWS began consolidating their programs, and they limited their relief operations. Since, like all private charities, they were being forced to increase the size of their grants to meet the higher level of support initiated by the Mothers' Aid program, they also limited the number of families they aided. To justify their limited relief operations, these charities emphasized their ability to guide clients toward self-sufficiency. For example, in a 1920 report the FWS said its work should not be "judged . . . by the number of families for which it is securing support, but by the number of families which it can so help that they are able to support themselves." Self-sufficiency, not dependency, remained the aim of their programs.[11]

In view of their new position in relation to public welfare and their desire to carve a niche of their own, the Protestant charities began insisting that "family welfare," and not merely relief, was their goal. The Associated Charities had long argued that their mission was "more than" relief, but they made their position clearer in 1920 when they changed their name to the Family Welfare Society. The leaders of the FWS said the name change would improve the public's perception of their activities: "The word 'charities' has lately come to signify material relief and with it accompanying stigma." More families, they added, would seek out their assistance if the association with charity were removed. The BPA had always had a less critical attitude toward relief, but in the 1920s, much like the FWS, it also began defining its services in terms of "family welfare." Family welfare included many of the same services these charities had always provided—financial aid, housing, employment referrals, food, and advice; however, beginning in the 1920s, these charities reflected a heightened consciousness about the need to coordinate services to ensure against destitution and to help families remain intact.[12]

Changes in the caseload of the charities also encouraged the shift toward family welfare. Before 1910, much of the relief and services the charities provided had aided widows, either elderly or with dependent children. As public welfare expanded in the 1920s and as unemployment worsened in Boston, families with unemployed or ill "breadwinners" made up the bulk of the cases. The stigma of an intact family needing aid—public or private—had weakened, and the Provident and the FWS, while resistant to providing financial assistance to these families, exhibited a new willingness to provide services to the families of the unemployed.[13]

Changes in their caseload was not alone, however, in the drive toward family welfare. With a larger number of trained social workers on their staffs, Boston's Protestant charity organizations, more than the Catholic and Jewish organizations, took a psychiatric approach to their work. Psychiatric social work—largely spearheaded at Smith College of Social Work in western Massachusetts—linked poverty to psychiatric disability or mental illness among the poor. The advocates of this approach recommended individual or group counseling as a corrective for the difficulties encountered by poor families. Influenced by these ideas, Boston's Protestant charity leaders began to discuss the difficulties of the poor in psychological terms related to "personal adjustment" or "sound family life." In this vein, Jeffrey R. Brackett of the FWS wrote in 1922, "Pauperism is a condition of mind not of poverty in things." Focusing on the unemployed breadwinner, he continued, "There cannot be real improvement in a man's condition unless he feels within himself at least the will to try for it." Need was no longer necessarily reserved for the poor; any family could experience a poverty "condition."[14]

In their discussion of "family welfare," the leaders of the BPA and the FWS combined the ideas of psychiatric social work with the rhetoric and practice of the "Americanization" movement popular at the time. Identifying the native-born family as the norm, they suggested that the poor and immigrants faced economic difficulties because they were not properly adjusting to American values, both mentally and behaviorally. In one study commissioned by the FWS in 1924 and titled "Family Problems in Immigrant Groups," the "causes of destitution and poverty" were related to the failure of immigrants to "adjust" to America. Specifically, it argued that "the contrast between national traditions and hereditary mentality of immigrants and the American environment contributed to their poor economic conditions." Thus, these Protestant charity leaders used notions of an "affectionate" family to criticize immigrant families that they described as "patriarchal."[15]

However, even as these charities attempted to assure cultural conformity by setting up the native-born Protestant family as normative, they often discussed changing gender relations as potentially beneficial to family structure. They argued that new relations between husbands and wives and between husbands and children were creating new family forms and that charities needed to recognize this development. In 1920, leaders of the FWS commented in their *Annual Report:* "In the old propriety family the husband had absolute control over his wife, even to the taking of her life. So, also in the matter of the children, the father was all-powerful. Today, with the emancipation of women, the husband is no longer the autocrat of the home. Brute force is no longer adequate to stabilize family life. With the man and woman today joining on equal terms for the establishment and maintenance of the home, there come new possibilities for better family life." With its large number of women staff members and volunteers, the FWS showed greater interest in issues related to women and gender relations than did the male leadership of the BPA. Nevertheless, the BPA leaders shared similar views of the "modern" family, saying that "affection" and not control should be the basis for family cohesion.[16]

The concept of the modern family advanced by these Protestant charity leaders reflected their belief in individualism and their tendency to see the family as a unit of individuals, all of whom had certain responsibilities and worth. While they never openly addressed the feminist potential of their ideas, these charities, more than Boston's Catholic and Jewish organizations, showed greater interest in the conditions of poor women. Moreover, they demonstrated greater acceptance of and support for working women even as they documented the poor conditions these women faced.[17]

In a study of working women in the late twenties, for example, the FWS discussed the double burden of working mothers: "Always, when a mother goes out to work . . . she is carrying on two professions, her outside job and that of homemaker." The report detailed the low wages these women earned, their difficulties getting to work, and the poor working conditions they faced, concluding that "to spend the entire day at work and then at night to wash the children's clothes, mend, scrub and bake, calls for a quiet sort of heroism which passes all unnoticed." The report, nevertheless, concluded that outside employment by mothers had "no noticeable effect upon the moral and spiritual welfare of the children," and even suggested that, in some cases, wage work gave women a more "optimistic" outlook since it lightened the financial burden of the family. The Catholic and Jewish charities took a more conservative position on women as they redefined their activities during the 1920s.[18]

The Catholic Charitable Bureau had been initially suspicious of the enlarged role for public welfare embodied in the Mothers' Aid Act. But, unlike the Protestant charities' fiscal concerns about the growth of public welfare, the CCB's suspicion had centered on the increased power that the Mothers' Aid program would give the Overseers of the Poor. Aware of the Protestant charity leaders' role in the drafting of the Mothers' Aid bill, the Bureau initially viewed the program, much as it viewed most public welfare measures at the time, as being controlled by Protestants. Accordingly, the Bureau took steps to provide its own relief to Catholic widows with dependent children. The CCB became more supportive of the Mothers' Aid program when a

Catholic woman was appointed to direct the program on the state level. By the early twenties, the Bureau's director was crediting the program with providing the financial support to keep children with their mothers and, specifically, to keep Catholic children in Catholic homes.[19]

Just as the Bureau became more accepting of the Mothers' Aid program, it supported other enlargements of public aid during the 1920s. Unlike the Protestant charities, the Bureau did not express reservations about the expanded public relief programs of the period. Moreover, it supported proposals for an old age pension. Speaking at a public hearing in 1923, Father George P. O'Conor, director of the CCB, described these pensions as "the duty of the state." Unlike the Protestant charity establishment, the CCB was optimistic about the expansion of public welfare programs and uncritical about potential "dependency" on these new programs. Bragging about its own services and new public initiatives, the CCB reported that "every generally acknowledged form of dependency from infancy to old age" was finally being addressed. Moreover, in discussing the Bureau's relief program, its directors did not make distinctions between public and private charity. They regularly referred widows and elderly cases to the Overseers during this time, without the elaborate justifications that were so common among Protestant charity leaders.[20]

The Bureau also displayed a more positive attitude toward working with the public welfare department than did the Protestant agencies. In 1924, the Bureau's director reported that "the most cordial and helpful relations exist between the Public Welfare Department and the Catholic Charitable Bureau," and expressed a willingness to work with public welfare officials. The Bureau eagerly sought, and received, space in the new municipal health clinics opened during Mayor Curley's second administration (1922–26). Likewise, when the old Charity Building was renovated—another Curley project—the CCB was given space in that building.[21]

Several factors explain the Bureau's growing support for public welfare programs and the increasing cooperation between the CCB and the public welfare department. First, the Bureau sensed that the governement was no longer beyond the reach of Catholic influence. During the 1910s, Mayors Fitzgerald and Curley had made Catholic appointments to the city's Board of Overseers, and Governor Walsh had changed the composition of the State Board of Charity. "Catholic influence," as the Bureau called Catholic political leadership, continued to widen during the 1920s as Catholic politicians made further inroads at the city and state level. The CCB did not endorse particular political candidates but exerted considerable informal influence through lobbying activities on specific policies.[22]

The CCB also sensed popular support for public welfare programs. Increasingly, Boston Catholics had begun to view public aid not as a source of shameful dependency but, instead, as a necessary resource in time of need. The Bureau's director commented on this sentiment even as he expressed reservations: "In these days, it is very necessary that we appear never indifferent to popular proposals for the promotion of public welfare. We may not feel that every such proposal deserves our support, but at least our refusal to support such proposals must not be lacking in sympathy. There is at present a perfect riot of statutory and legislative proposals along social welfare lines, and the end is not yet." As in the past, the Bureau monitored welfare legislation and gauged the popular appeal of public programs, but the Bureau also increasingly endorsed legislation that would enlarge public welfare functions, such as the popular proposals for an old age pension.[23]

The Bureau's desire to limit the influence of Protestant charities also motivated its increased support for public programs. With Catholics gaining greater political control, the CCB viewed the enlargement of public programs as a means of consolidating their gains. In 1922, the director wrote that he hoped the Bureau would be able to aid all Catholic children "that are not under the supervision of the State or City Department of Public Welfare." The implication was that public supervision of children no longer posed a threat, or, at least, not as great a threat as the private Protestant agencies. In addition, enlarged programs in public relief had the potential of lessening the need for Catholics to rely on Protestant charities for assistance. Understood in this way, Catholic support for public welfare in the 1920s was an expression of cultural resistance even as it indicated assimilation.[24]

Unlike the Protestant charities that were consolidating their activities during the 1920s, the CCB expanded its operations in and around Boston during this period. The Bureau opened neighborhood houses, modeled after the city's Protestant-led settlement houses. In addition to offering educational and recreation programs, the Bureau's neighborhood centers became outposts for its relief operations, which were also expanding. Since the Bureau relied on nuns and other uncertified women "visitors," it did not face the increased salary costs that the Protestant charities did at this time. Moreover, while Protestant and Jewish charities were relying increasingly on donations, the CCB benefited from regular infusions of cash from the Archdiocese.[25]

Like the Protestant charities, the CCB began to refer to its programs as family welfare during the 1920s, and, like them, it began to offer counseling and advice programs for families. Historian Susan Walton, who has investigated the history of Catholic charity in Boston, sees the CCB's increased focus on family welfare as an effort by the Church to exert more control over poor Catholics, a more ethnically mixed group than Boston's Irish-dominated Archdiocese. She also relates the trend toward family welfare to increased class stratification among Boston's Catholic population; she argues that more economically secure Catholics saw family welfare programs as a means of instilling "middle-class values" among less fortunate Catholics while defending the "respectability" of Catholics in general. The effort cut both ways, according to Walton, since it was both a criticism of the poor and a defense of Catholics against similar criticism from "without."[26]

However, the Bureau's family welfare program differed considerably from similarly named programs of the BPA and the FWS. Unlike these Protestant charities, the Bureau did not readily accept the notions of psychiatric social work. In fact, the Bureau's director often warned the agencies under his control against the influence of professional social work practices. Associating professional social work with what he called "the so-called non-sectarian private societies," the director saw it as a Protestant threat. For the directors of the CCB, the need for "family adjustment" was related to a weakening of religious faith and not to mental defects. Reacting against the emerging social work profession and its emphasis on psychological adjustment, the CCB's director organized a lecture series for the Bureau's visitors. This program, which in the 1930s developed into a social work program at Boston College, focused on ways to connect the CCB's work more directly to Catholic doctrine and beliefs. Nevertheless, these courses encouraged Catholics to take the civil service exams for positions in public social service programs.[27]

The Bureau's view on family relations also differed from that of the Protestant charities. Its directors shared none of the Protestant charities' latent feminist analysis of gender relations and saw changing family relations as a threat to social stability. They considered men the "proper" heads of families and insisted that the Bureau's programs would not interfere with male prerogative. "The CCB," wrote its director in 1926, "does not aim to take from any one the privilege of planning for his own family or even of bearing his own burdens." While the Bureau recognized that many poor families relied on the wages of two parents, it saw the wage work of women as something to be avoided. Moreover, it counseled against the use of birth control and divorce, practices it accused the Protestant agencies of supporting. Thus, while the Bureau, like the Protestant organizations, adopted a family-services approach, it approached that work quite differently from its Protestant counterparts, stressing not individuality but rather family interdependency and the male prerogative to head the family. This approach simultaneously reenforced premodern gender relations within the family while describing the Catholic family in terms of the modern nuclear unit. As with other aspects of Boston Catholicism, the family welfare work of the CCB was a combination of cultural resistance and accommodation.[28]

Boston's Jewish charities, organized within the Federated Jewish Charities (FJC), had endorsed the expansion of public welfare earlier and more enthusiastically than either Catholic or Protestant charity organizations. The city's Jewish charity organizations had always had a cordial relationship with the Overseers, and a Jewish representative had served on the Overseers' board since the late nineteenth century. In the teens and twenties, Simon E. Hecht filled that position, and after more than ten years on the board commanded considerable leverage. Under the direction of Martha Michaels Silverman, the Federated, as well as its chief relief agency, the United Hebrew Benevolent Association (UHBA), had supported the passage of the widows' subsidy plan. When the Mothers' Aid law passed in 1913, the UHBA referred all eligible cases to the Overseers. Silverman as well as other leaders within the Federated argued that the public welfare department was better equipped to provide long-term support to poor mothers with children. In 1919, the Welfare Committee of the Federated insisted that the Mothers' Aid Act had resulted in a "marked improvement in the homes of those receiving this relief" and pointed to Mothers' Aid as evidence that legislation to expand public welfare was beneficial.[29]

However, the leaders of the Federated took a more tempered position regarding the expansion of public welfare than the CCB did. While they regularly noted that the temporary aid provided to the unemployed was not sufficient and advocated broader assistance to the unemployed, they did not think that the Overseers were necessarily responsible for providing aid to the unemployed. Likewise, they did not endorse the old age pension proposals that were circulating during the 1920s. They were not as strongly opposed to them as the Protestant charity leaders, but like their Protestant counterparts, they considered these plans, particularly those not requiring contributions from wage earners, as potentially expensive to taxpayers. They did, however, support the idea of public assistance for the elderly, and the UHBA transferred many of its elderly cases to the Overseers long before the Old Age Assistance program was enacted in 1930.[30]

For Jewish charity leaders, public aid represented only a base of support which Jewish private charities would supplement, and they insisted that Jewish charity officials continue to serve as caseworkers for any Jewish recipients of public aid—an idea that the Overseers resisted. The Federated eventually worked out an agreement with the Overseers by promising that it would transfer only "permanent cases" and not families "temporarily" in need because of unemployment. In practice, the Federated continued to work with both temporary and permanent cases making little distinction between these groups. The Federated did not rank private aid as superior to public aid or consider public aid particularly unsuited for the unemployed. Its leaders saw a good working relation with the Overseers as being to their advantage, though, and drew distinctions among cases in order to foster agreement. When Maurice Hexter, a Harvard graduate, succeeded Silverman, tensions lessened between the Overseers and the Federated. In 1919, Hexter reported, "In the work of caring for the relief necessities of our families, we have enjoyed a fine spirit of cooperation with the Overseers of the Poor, from whom appreciable allotments for our families are received." Throughout the 1920s, Jewish charity officials worked closely with the Overseers on initial cases and on policy issues that might affect Jewish recipients of aid.[31]

In their own dealings with poor families, the Federated's leaders stressed the need to combine relief with social services such as employment referral, medical aid, and family counseling; however, they did not share the Protestant charities' criticism of relief as potentially debilitating. To the Protestant charity leadership, relief led to "dependency," but the leaders of the Federated argued that relief was "a means for reestablishing independence." Accordingly, they increased relief expenditures throughout the 1920s.[32]

Like the CCB, the Federated expanded its operations during the 1920s, opening five "District Service Centers" in various neighborhoods. The Federated envisioned the neighborhood centers as a democratic and locally responsive program aimed at bringing the city's newer Jewish residents, mainly immigrants from Russia and Eastern Europe, together with older German Jewish families. Part of a general reorganization, the District Centers combined the relief efforts of various smaller Jewish charities, including the United Hebrew Benevolent Association, and established the Federated as the central source of private relief for Jewish families. Unlike the Catholic neighborhood centers, the Jewish District Service Centers were staffed by "experienced" social workers, many of them women with formal training in social work. The social workers at the centers played a more vocal role in policy making than their counterparts in the Protestant and Catholic organizations and enjoyed a fair amount of independence in their work.[33]

The District Service Centers blended professional social work with an effort to build a strong and unified Jewish community in Boston. Thus, while the social workers at the centers fully embraced the casework methodology and used the language of psychiatric social work in their discussions of their recipients, they did not display the us-them attitude of the social workers employed by the FWS and the BPA. Moreover, the Federated purposely combined the relief activities of the District Service Centers with recreational and educational programs to make the centers places for all Jews, not only those in financial need.

Since the District Service Centers referred "traditional" relief cases—the elderly and widows with dependent children—to the Overseers, nearly half of their relief cases involved married men with children. In addition to financial assistance, usually larger than the assistance distributed by either Protestant or Catholic charities, these families received employment referrals, medical services, and children's services such as summer camp and educational scholarships. The Federated saw the two-parent family as the best protection against poverty, and Federated services were aimed at maintaining intact families. The Federated sought ways to assure that the father's wage was sufficient to support the family and provided employment assistance and wage subsidies.[34]

Focusing on "normal" families, defined as "husband, wife, and children," the District social workers showed less interest in the conditions of poor women without families than their Protestant counterparts did. While they drew the relationship between the breakdown of families and poverty, they did not relate it specifically to the experience of women and children. One social worker, for example, commented the weakening of the "patriarchal aspect" of the family affected family relations, but she did not connect those changes to the economic and political behavior of women. In fact, she considered the weakening of religious observations more significant to changes in the family—changes she implied were for the worse.[35]

As much as it sought to shore up the "normal" family, the Federated was less guarded than the CCB about family relations. Unlike the CCB, the Federated did not oppose either birth control or divorce, though it viewed the latter as a potential cause of economic hardship. While the Federated preferred that married women with children stay at home, it did not discourage married women who chose to work from seeking employment outside the home, especially if their children were older. In fact, the Federated employed married women as social workers, pointing to their personal knowledge of family issues.

The Federated's expansion during the 1920s proved expensive. As Boston's more economically secure Jewish population began shifting away from the center city neighborhoods, the Federated lost much of its base of support. At the same time, the expenses of the District Service Centers were increasing, in part because of demands by the social workers for higher salaries. Facing mounting deficits, the Federated reorganized in 1929 and hired a new director, Ben M. Selekman, who had a Ph.D. in economics and experience on the research staff of the Russell Sage Foundation in New York. Under his direction, the Federated moved away from its decentralized organization and regrouped as the Associated Jewish Philanthropies (AJP). The AJP moved Jewish charity in Boston closer to the Protestant model of charity and social services. Stressing philanthropic endeavors, the AJP moved away from direct assistance to the poor. The social services formerly provided at the district level were centralized in the Jewish Family Welfare Association (FWA). Much like its Protestant counterparts, the FWA saw its goals as family "reconstruction and rehabilitation," more than financial assistance.[36]

In two important ways, however, the AJP and the FWA differed from Boston's Protestant charities. First, the AJP, like the Federated before it, remained committed to building and protecting Boston's Jewish community, and its family welfare program had an optimistic attitude about the potential economic and personal success of Jewish families. For example, while Protestant charities regularly published photographs and descriptions of their worst cases in their reports, the FWA included success stories and photographs of happy Jewish families in its publications. Stressing family success, FWA leaders expressed their belief in human potential rather than the distrust of the poor that was so evident in the literature of Protestant charities of the time.[37]

The AJP also differed from the BPA and the FWS in increasingly seeing public assistance as a legitimate source of financial aid for the elderly and the unemployed. By the late 1920s, Boston Jewish charity leaders joined in the effort to secure an old age pension, and they recommended that the unemployed use public aid if necessary. Unlike their Protestant counterparts, the leaders of the Jewish FWA did not think that extensive casework methodology needed to accompany public aid. The FWA would simply assist those families in need of special assistance or supervision. Jewish charity leaders believed that members of the same faith were better able to address these families' needs than public aid officials. Unlike the Protestant charity leaders, the Jewish FWA did not eagerly attempt to reform or to control the enlarging public welfare program in Boston. The FWA used it instead.

Move toward Cooperation

As the city's Protestant, Catholic, and Jewish charity organizations reoriented themselves toward an enlarging public welfare program, a movement for greater cooperation among private agencies was also developing. Although a number of cooperative welfare organizations sprang up in the teens and the twenties, the Council of Social Agencies (CSA) became the leading interagency organization in Boston during the 1920s. Spearheaded by leaders of the Protestant charities, the CSA was a reaction against both the enlargement of public welfare and the social and political changes that were weakening the dominance of Protestant charities within the city's charity system.[38]

The CSA began with "a few regulars," primarily white male directors of private agencies and settlement houses. The earliest members included Robert A. Woods of the South End House, Jeffrey R. Brackett of the Simmons School of Social Work, and William H. Pear of the Provident. These founders expressed concern about three things: the enlargement of public welfare; the "politicization" of welfare, by which they meant the control of city government by Irish politicians; and the increased costs that the leading Protestant charities were facing. Incorporated in 1922, the CSA's charter membership list covered the spectrum of social welfare agencies in Boston, including the Overseers, the major Protestant organizations, the Catholic Charitable Bureau, and the Federated Jewish Charities. However, the majority of the officeholders and executive committee members were Yankee Protestants and leaders of the BPA and the FWS. In addition, the Protestant agencies paid a larger share of the CSA's operating expenses during its early years, when dues were less formally calculated, and representatives of Protestant-led social service agencies wrote most of the reports in the CSA's monthly *Bulletin*.[39]

Although the CSA presented itself as an information sharing organization, it advanced a vision of social services much in keeping with the ideas of the Protestant charities. The CSA opposed the rapid enlargement of public welfare, associating it with corruption and inefficiency, and called for administrative reforms to curb the department's growth. Making formal recommendations to Mayor Nichols in 1929, the CSA urged that the department be managed more tightly through a smaller Board of Overseers and a larger staff. The CSA also stressed the need for professional casework methodology for all public relief cases, not just Mothers' Aid cases, and recommended that the department employ more trained caseworkers to assure the "careful examination" of applicants. As a consultant on public welfare, the CSA proved largely ineffective. Twelve members continued to make up the voluntary Overseers board instead of the seven recommended by the CSA report, and casework methodology continued to be applied most extensively to Mothers' Aid cases. Moreover, the CSA efforts were stymied by City Council resistance to efforts to reform the department's operations.

The CSA's ability to forge cooperation among private charities was more successful. As the twenties progressed, the CSA's membership grew, and Catholic and Jewish charities took a more active role in the organization. By 1924, the CSA's executive committee included the directors of both the Catholic and Jewish charitable organizations, and in 1925, Reverend George P. O'Conor, director of the Catholic Charitable Bureau, became vice president. Despite being a vehicle of ethnic assimilation, the CSA was slow to invite black social service leaders to join the organization, leaving it open to charges of racial segregation in 1931; CSA officials denied the accusations. The instance, nevertheless, drives home how marginalized Boston's small black population remained and how dominant white Protestants and white ethnics remained in carving out public and private charity policies in the 1920s.[40]

But even as Catholic and Jewish charity leaders became active in the CSA, they showed different attitudes toward their participation. Well into the 1920s, the CCB director expressed suspicion about the CSA's Protestant leadership. In his report to the archbishop, he justified his membership, saying, "In this way, he [the director of the CCB] is in touch with the trend of things, and is forewarned of possible dangers to the Catholic cause," adding that this was "particularly true in the question of legislation, much of which originates" from such organizations. His comments reflected resistance as much as assimilation. Members of the Federated, in contrast, did not view the CSA as a particular threat to their operations, though, like the CCB, they were careful to establish boundaries regarding their participation. The Federated, for example, had its own fund-raising program and strongly opposed city-wide funding plans, like Community Chests, an idea that many Protestant members of the CSA supported.[41]

Over the course of the decade, the relationship between the city's Catholic, Jewish, and Protestant charity leaders became less strained. The CSA provided a meeting ground for representatives from the largest relief agencies, and together they shared ideas about the enlargement of public welfare and their new role as social service providers. As members of the "family welfare department" of the CSA, they exchanged ideas and information. Although representatives from the Protestant charities dominated the welfare discussion, Catholic and Jewish representatives became more vocal and active as the decade continued. The result was a greater emphasis on poverty as a family issue rather than as an individual failing. While this approach broadened the scope and activities of private charities and lessened the tendency, particularly among Protestant charities, to assign individual blame for economic failure, it muted the discussion of the particular needs of poor women. The emphasis on poverty as a family issue also tended to focus attention on maintaining two-parent families and particularly on assuring the wages of male breadwinners. The cooperation among Boston's Catholic, Jewish, and Protestant agencies in the CSA did not, however, unify their different perspectives on the growing public welfare program. As a result, there was no clear bifurcation between public and private welfare even as public welfare programs were overshadowing the work of private charities. As the crisis of the thirties unfolded, the growing consensus among private charities on the importance of family welfare as well as the persisting differences between and among Boston's public and private charities would complicate the development of welfare policy in Boston.

5 THE THIRTIES

THE PROLONGED and widespread Depression of the 1930s put unprecedented demands on Boston's public and private relief agencies, precipitating the surrender of relief efforts by the private agencies and the permanent enlargement of public welfare operations. The expansion of public welfare during the 1930s, however, was not a *deus ex machina*, prompted by the economic emergency alone. It evolved out of earlier welfare practices and ongoing debates about poor relief. Moreover, the expansion of welfare during the 1930s, like earlier expansion, was gendered. Less oppositional than earlier, the welfare politics of the 1930s produced an enlarged public assistance program, focused largely on the needs of unemployed men. The narrowing of the political discussion to the unemployment crisis meant that issues related to general relief, aid for the elderly, and programs for women with dependent children went unaddressed in the local political discussion even as New Deal legislation introduced special programs for the elderly and dependent children. Thus, although the Depression and the New Deal created new welfare policies and programs, they did not produce a consensus about the purpose or function of public assistance. The political consensus that did emerge surrounded the appropriateness of aiding unemployed men with families. This represented a significant shift from the nineteenth-century vision of welfare as the site of last resort, but it did not guarantee long-term political support for social provisions to people in need. What it did do, however, was affirm the male-headed family as the ideal unit and encourage policy formation in terms of aid to families in need.[1]

In many ways, the scale of the economic emergency as well as the federal intervention after 1932 differentiated the welfare policy of the 1930s from earlier program developments. The amount of public and private relief dispensed in the first three years of the Depression alone far surpassed all the relief expenditures of the previous decade. Moreover, the welfare programs of the New Deal dispensed federal funds to the needy for the first time and established federally funded categorical relief programs for the elderly and dependent children. Despite their scope, however, the welfare policies of the 1930s did not represent a break from the past, but, instead, evolved out of earlier policy developments. Likewise, no ideological consensus about support for the poor emerged during the thirties. Protestant, Catholic, and Jewish charity leaders continued to exhibit markedly different approaches to dispensing relief; while they, like most Americans, concurred that public initiative and funds were necessary to stem the crisis of the Depression, they demonstrated varying levels of support for federal programs. The relief programs of the New Deal, like their precursors, were implemented in the crucible of local politics, ensuring the creation of a disjointed public assistance program. Much as during the previous two decades, the expansion of public welfare during the 1930s was the product of political compromise, a blending of ideas and practices. The outcome should not be judged, however, against some idealized notion of "New Deal liberalism." The welfare programs established during the 1930s were the product of contested ideas and practices about relief played out among Boston's private and public relief organization in the context of local politics. These local struggles and disputes, and not some abstract rejection or failure of liberalism, established "welfare" as we know it today, an incoherent patchwork of social provisions both celebrated and disparaged.[2]

Impact of the Depression

Boston's economy did not experience a sudden crisis or collapse with the onset of the Depression, but rather a gradual stagnation that was deep and prolonged. In many ways, the economic difficulties of the twenties tempered the city for the crisis of the thirties. Boston had not seen much of the wild prosperity and boom of the twenties and so the initial blow of the Crash was not as severe. Moreover, the diversified economy of this commercial city protected it from the sudden collapse experienced in urban centers where the economies were based on manufacturing. Although panic was felt on State Street, the business and banking section of downtown, 1929 marked more the beginning of a gradual slide downward than an abrupt drop. Gradually, however, as the manufacturing output of the region bottomed out, Boston was pulled down. Between 1929 and 1933, wholesale figures in Boston fell 57 percent, nearly 3 percent worse than in other large cities, and the number of full-time employees in wholesaling decreased by nearly half, a situation worse than in comparable cities. Though retail sales remained stronger than in other urban areas, they still fell over 40 percent. By 1932, Boston had joined most other large cities in registering 30 percent unemployment in the trades. This, combined with large numbers of underemployed workers, meant that half of the workforce—between 130,000 and 150,000 people—saw their wages drop or disappear.[3]

As elsewhere, the hardship of the unfolding Depression was distributed unevenly. People from the poorer sections of the city experienced four to five times the joblessness rates of those in "better" neighborhoods. Italians in the North End and East Boston and Irish in the South End and Charlestown suffered higher than average unemployment, as did Boston's black population concentrated in the South End and Roxbury. More prosperous Irish and Jewish residents of the outskirts—Brighton, Jamaica Plain, and West Roxbury—suffered less than their counterparts in the urban core, and, as during earlier economic downturns, the Yankee residents of the Back Bay experienced the lowest level of unemployment.[4]

With its network of public and private charity organizations, Boston, unlike many cities, had the institutional structure to aid many of the victims of the economic crisis. During the first year of the Depression alone, public relief payments increased 47 percent, and the caseload jumped from 7,463 to 11,478. By 1932, the annual caseload had soared to 28,824, with one out of four unemployed workers being aided. Only Milwaukee and Chicago carried higher monthly public caseloads per 10,000 people. Boston's per capita expenditures on both public and private relief also far exceeded the national average, as did its public welfare grant size.[5]

Despite Boston's comparatively strong safety net, less than half of the city's unemployed received public or private aid, leaving thousands of the jobless to rely on whatever savings they might have or on the generosity of their relatives and friends. Those able to get relief received less than a subsistence level of income, estimated in the mid-thirties to be $15 a week for a family of four. Families of four who qualified for public aid received between $9 and $10 per week, and private charities provided between $4 and $9 to families per week. Boston residents most affected by the Depression were already poor, and for them the situation was bleak. Reporting to Harry Hopkins in 1934, field agent Martha Gellhorn wrote: "The picture is so grim that whatever words I use will seem hysterical and exaggerated." While the city had few breadlines and no evidence of homeless in the streets, the households of the unemployed were filled with "fear, fear driving them into a state of semi-collapse; cracking nerves; and an overpowering terror of the future."[6]

The profile of the "typical" relief recipient changed during the 1930s, and unemployed men became the largest group receiving aid from the city's public and private charities. In 1928, 1,598 Dependent Aid cases were attributed to unemployment; by 1933, that figure had risen to 30,229. As the unemployed swelled the welfare rolls, they overshadowed the other types of public relief cases, and political debate about welfare was transformed into a debate about unemployment assistance. Whereas in the teens, the image of the "worthy widow" had dominated the political debate over welfare, the debate about welfare in the 1930s concerned the needs of families, described as an unemployed father, a wife, and children. Even in the labeling of some cases as "unworthy" or "undeserving," the criticism was of men who worked on the side while receiving benefits and, thus, robbing other men of the funds they needed to "to support their wives and children."[7]

The public enumeration and discussion of the unemployed on welfare was new. In earlier periods, the unemployed had used the public welfare covertly. Public welfare was popularly understood to be the source of aid to the indigent, the poor elderly, and widowed mothers, and, by and large, that is what it was. With the widespread unemployment of the thirties, however, public welfare began special efforts to aid families of the unemployed, a focus that gave priority to the needs of male "breadwinners." Private relief agencies, likewise, saw their relief rolls swell with the unemployed.

Most of the unemployed men on relief were between twenty-five and forty-five years old, married with children, never before dependent on public aid. A quarter of the private relief applicants and almost 40 percent of the public relief applicants were new to the relief rolls. Manual workers made up the largest percentage of the unemployed on relief, as they had before the Depression; however, the relief recipients of the early thirties represented a larger range of occupational backgrounds, including skilled workers—carpenters, painters, plumbers, bricklayers—and even clerical and professional workers. The previous wages among these unemployed men had ranged from $15 to $40 a week, but most had been between $25 and $35, a wage level considered "adequate" at the time. These new recipients of public aid had not been chronically poor or underemployed as had earlier applicants for assistance.[8]

Women also experienced unemployment during the 1930s; however, the structure of outdoor relief hid this. Married women living with their husbands were aided as part of a male-headed household, and women with dependents, if they qualified, were usually helped through the Mothers' Aid program. Although the women in both situations might also have been unemployed, they were not listed as such. The few women listed as "unemployed" on the relief rolls had skills and economic backgrounds more typical of "traditional" public relief recipients. Most of them had worked as domestics or restaurant employees; some had been factory workers. Information on their previous wages was not collected, but their occupational backgrounds suggest that they had earned considerably less than the unemployed men in the survey, probably between $5 and $10 a week. Like the men, all unemployed women on relief had dependents. Unmarried women, in general, were not eligible for relief unless they were elderly.[9]

As larger numbers of unemployed men turned to public aid, the ethnic and racial composition of public relief recipients also changed. A greater percentage of public and private relief went to native-born individuals than it had during the twenties, and this trend continued each year. In part a reflection of the decreasing numbers of foreign-born residents in Boston because of immigration restrictions of the previous decade, this change also indicated the wider use of relief by groups not previously likely to depend on public assistance. Along with the "Americanizing" of the relief rolls, shifts occurred in the ethnic and racial groups represented among the unemployed on public assistance. Among the foreign-born on relief, the Irish, who had earlier made up the majority of foreign-born relief cases, comprised only 17 percent whereas Italians made up 40 percent, a disproportionate amount to their percentage in the city's foreign-born population. This shift reflected the improving social and economic opportunities for Boston's Irish and the dire poverty of many of its Italian residents. African Americans represented less than one-tenth of the unemployed on public assistance, but were counted separately for the first time during the 1930s, suggesting an increased, though still disproportionably low, use of public welfare by the city's black population.[10]

The expansion of public welfare, which had been so hotly contested during the 1920s, paled in the face of the demands of the Depression. The Overseers caseload more than quadrupled between 1928 and 1932, with 28,824 people receiving some type of public assistance that year. The department's expenditures on poor relief increased by even a larger amount, growing over 400 percent between 1929 and 1933, reaching nearly $13.6 million that year. Composing a third of the city's budget, public aid had become the single largest expense Boston faced. The number of unemployed seeking aid overwhelmed the city's public and private charities. Hundreds of families arrived daily at the Charity Building on Hawkins Street either to apply to the Overseers for relief or to seek assistance from the private agencies housed there. The long wait and the crowded conditions were so bad that the Charity Building became known as the "House of Horrors." Any "capable" man receiving public aid was required to check in at Hawkins Street four days a week and to be put to work if possible. The assignments were few, though, and the city's wood yard, which was next to the Charity Building and which had long employed many male recipients of public assistance, could use only so many. As a consequence, men often checked in at Hawkins Street only to be told to go home. So overwhelmed by the demands of unemployed men, the Overseers asked that Mothers' Aid recipients no longer come to the Hawkins Street headquarters, and for the first time in the city's history, Mothers' Aid recipients were sent monthly checks. Private charities began to "lend" visitors to the public welfare department, but as new applicants were taken on, caseloads continued to increase. The city's public and private charities scrambled to formulate welfare policy in response to the unfolding crisis of the Depression. In doing so, they relied on a mixture of ideas and past practices, ensuring a makeshift response to the emergency and contributing to a fragmented public assistance program.[11]

Private Charities Respond

With the local and national emphasis on voluntarism during the early thirties, the Protestant, Catholic, and Jewish charitable organizations were under pressure to distribute as much relief as possible. Alarmed by the rapid increase in public expenditures, Boston's fiscally conservative business organizations, including the Chamber of Commerce, rallied the private agencies to increase their relief efforts. Dominated by Republicans, the city's business community supported the Hoover administration's emphasis on voluntarism and private relief efforts. The businessmen opposed any public unemployment program and pressured the city's private charities and the Council of Social Agencies to organize a combined fund-raising campaign to aid the unemployed. The result was an explosion in private relief expenditures between 1929 and 1932. While these expenditures remained well below the level of public relief, the increase in private expenditures was twice the increase in public welfare expenditures.[12]

Much like the public relief effort in the early years of the Depression, the work of Boston's private charities during these years focused primarily on the needs of unemployed men. These organizations had transferred most of their "long-term" cases to public welfare before the Depression, and they had begun to redefine their work as family welfare. While the crisis of the Depression moved these organizations back toward relief activities, they did not resume the support of "traditional" poor relief cases, widows with children or elderly. The private charities defined the assistance they gave to unemployed men both as temporary and as part of their larger family welfare programs. As during the 1920s, however, differences between these private charities persisted even as their activities began to converge. The various approaches of these agencies to unemployment relief reflected the underlying philosophical differences among these charities as well as differences in the clients they served. However, the inconsistent and, at times, contradictory relief policies toward the unemployed also reflected general disagreements about the best way to provide relief to male breadwinners. Aid to families, as opposed to individuals, had become the focus of welfare policy.

During the Depression, the Catholic Charitable Bureau continued to view charity as a means of maintaining the ties of poor Catholics to the Church. Perhaps even more than earlier, the CCB emphasized the "spiritual" influence of its effort during the 1930s. Working at the neighborhood level, the Bureau aided thousands of Catholics, many of whom had been poor before the Depression. The Bureau did not emphasize its relief effort toward the unemployed, describing its work as aid to families. In order to maximize its potential contact, the Bureau gave smaller grants to a larger number of families. As earlier, the Bureau did not view relief as necessarily contributing to the eventual self-sufficiency or independence of its clients, nor did it see charity as creating any unwarranted dependency. Likewise, the Bureau did not attach work requirements to its aid and did not insist that charity be earned.[13]

Boston's Jewish charities also increased their relief efforts during the early thirties but took a different approach to unemployment relief than the CCB. While Jewish charities also stressed family assistance, they placed greater emphasis on the "special" needs of the unemployed male "breadwinner" during this time of economic crisis. Unlike the CCB, the Jewish Family Welfare Association distributed larger grants to a smaller number of families. The FWA believed that its aid could help families become self-sufficient and saw "adequate" support as the best means of making that possible. These grants, though larger than those from other private agencies or public welfare programs, were not tied to a work requirement. Viewing work relief as potentially insulting to male breadwinners, the FWA developed vocational training and job placement programs. These programs were restricted by design and by practice to unemployed men who had families to support.[14]

The leading Protestant charities, the Boston Provident Association and the Family Welfare Society, nearly doubled their relief expenditures between 1930 and 1933 as they set up special programs for the unemployed. Far less focused on family support, the Protestant charities stressed individual need during periods of unemployment. Reversing the downsizing both organizations had experienced during the twenties, the BPA and the FWS aided more people—men and women—than they ever had. Unlike Catholic and Jewish organizations, the Protestant agencies attempted to assist single men and women who were unemployed. The BPA and the FWS provided relief grants that were considerably larger than the aid from the CCB but not as large as the Jewish FWA's grants. The Protestant charities viewed their relief efforts as more than charity but, nevertheless, remained cautious since they believed that giving "too much" might encourage laziness and dependency. They placed work requirements, usually some type of day labor, on the unemployed whom they aided. Work relief, according to the leaders of the BPA and the FWS, ensured the "dignity" and "self-respect" of people. In practical terms, they also believed that work relief dissuaded "fakers" from applying for aid, especially if the work requirement was greater than the corresponding aid.[15]

The differences in unemployment assistance among the private charities were reproduced in governmental work relief programs of the 1930s. These programs vacillated between centralized and decentralized control and endlessly debated the definition of "adequate" support. Just as Boston's private charities were unclear about the relationship between work relief and direct relief, so too were the federally funded relief programs of the New Deal. Nevertheless, the focus on unemployed men that guided private relief would carry over into the public relief policies of the Depression.

Interagency organizations such as the Council of Social Agencies and professional social work organizations strove to make private charity operations more uniform during the early Depression years. The joint fundraising efforts and the eventual creation of the Community Federation of Boston in 1935 pressed private charities to adopt similar policies for public and private assistance. Since the Protestant charity and social work network dominated these organizations, their "uniform" programs reflected the Protestant charities' insistence on a limited amount of relief and a required work assignment whenever possible. But the inconsistency of policy, public and private, suggests that their efforts to shape welfare policy were only partially successful.[16]

By 1932, it had become clear that, despite their efforts, the private organizations could not adequately respond to the economic difficulties. Although joint fund-raising efforts had been initially successful, contributions became more difficult to collect as the Depression continued. With the large-scale use of public relief by the unemployed and calls for even further governmental action, the private charities took different positions on new public welfare programs—different from each other and, in some regards, different from their earlier positions.

While the CCB had, throughout the twenties, shown an increasing acceptance of an enlarged public welfare program—particularly one directed by Catholics—it showed less enthusiasm for further expansion of public welfare during the 1930s, particularly the introduction of federal welfare programs. The CCB's guarded attitude toward new welfare programs reflected the growing conservatism of the Church in Boston during the thirties as well as its suspicion that the new federal welfare programs might be beyond the reach of Catholic influence. While American Catholicism in other cities and even at the national level showed some evidence of a class analysis of the hardships of the Depression, the Boston Archdiocese rejected the social criticism of more radical Catholics during the 1930s. Catholics in Boston proved powerful supporters of FDR, but the Church in Boston showed only tempered support for the liberalism of the New Deal. Critical of many New Deal programs, the CCB leaders reported that the new welfare programs were "rigid" and accused them of not addressing the "spiritual" needs of the poor. Their criticism of public welfare—particularly federal welfare—did not prompt them to criticize expanded public benefits for Catholics, however. The CCB's mixed signals, though, fostered a guarded acceptance of enlarged public welfare programs even as those programs aided Catholics in the largest numbers.[17]

In contrast to the directors of the CCB, the leaders of Boston's Jewish charities strongly supported both the enlargement of public programs and the ideas of the New Deal. As they had earlier, they considered the public welfare department the proper source for relief; they referred cases there whenever possible and lent social workers to the department to help with the overwhelming caseload. By 1936, Jewish charity leaders, like the Jewish community as a whole, had swung to support Roosevelt and proved ardent supporters of his New Deal programs.[18]

The leaders of the city's Protestant charities underwent a sea change in attitudes during the 1930s. The resistance toward public welfare that remained among the Yankee representatives of the Protestant social welfare network was erased by the severity of the Depression. When the large-scale unemployment of the early thirties caused the budget of the public welfare department to skyrocket, they did not attack the increased expenditures as they had criticized the increases of the 1920s. Instead, they saw the explosion in public welfare expenditures as an opportunity to reform public welfare in Boston and called for the implementation of casework methodology, the determination of grants based on a family budget, and professional certification for all social workers. The resources of the leading Protestant charities, already weakened by the economic downturns of the 1920s, were nearly depleted by the collapse of the economy in the 1930s. Officials of organizations that had traditionally opposed public welfare, like the BPA and the FWS, conceded that "public welfare agencies must bear the burden of relief for some time to come." While it is unclear whether these leaders converted politically to the Roosevelt cause, it is clear that after his election they supported the New Deal programs. Many of them were, in fact, appointed by the Roosevelt administration to oversee federal relief programs in the state.[19]

With the advent of the New Deal, public welfare was established as the primary source of aid to the poor and unemployed. Almost immediately after Roosevelt's election, private relief decreased, falling by half between 1932 and 1933. By legislation, no private agency was allowed to distribute public moneys or to administer the work relief programs of the New Deal. This New Deal ruling brought to a close the "informal" interaction between public and private charities that had long been the rule in Boston, especially between the Protestant charities and the Overseers. As the public welfare programs expanded, space at the Charity Building became tight, forcing the private charities housed there to find new locations and ending the association between public and private charities set in place during the nineteenth century. By 1939, the "House of Horrors" had become solely the public welfare department.[20]

Political Debate

Just as private charities took new turns while clinging to old ways so too did the politics of welfare in the city. During the 1920s, the political debate surrounding expansion of public welfare had divided largely along ethnic lines, pitting native-born Republican councilmen against Irish Democrats. The latter, in turn, were divided among themselves politically but were unified in their efforts to make public welfare more responsive to the city's poor. During that time, the debate over welfare centered on two issues: the level of city expenditures on poor relief and the administration of the public welfare department. On both issues, Irish Democrats on the City Council criticized the city's Overseers of the Poor for their tightfisted approach to caring for the poor. Representing the poorer sections of the city, areas with heavy immigrant concentration, these City Council representatives, along with the Curley administration of 1922–26, approved larger appropriations of public welfare and regularly implored the employees of the public welfare department to treat the poor with more dignity and respect. In addition, several City Council leaders argued for less severe investigation and supervision of welfare recipients. The Republican members of the City Council largely disagreed with their Irish Democratic colleagues, and they struggled, unsuccessfully, to limit the budget of the public welfare department during this time, especially during the administrations of mayors Peters (1918–22) and Nichols (1926–30).

The political debate over public welfare that began during the 1920s intensified during the 1930s. As the welfare rolls and expenditures rose, City Council members engaged in heated debates over the purposes, function, and administration of the municipal welfare program. The political debate over these issues, however, did not set immigrant politicians against the Yankee native-born leaders of the city, as in the 1920s, but instead divided ethnic politicians among themselves. While the Irish still dominated city government, they were no more unified than the Democratic Party at the state level, and Curley's controversial administrations as mayor in the early thirties and as governor in the mid-thirties further divided local politicians. Moreover, as other ethnic groups—Jews, Italians, and Syrians—won a voice in city government and as Irish Bostonians with middle-class aspirations began to build alliances with Republicans and Yankee reformers, the welfare debate became less stratified in terms of class and ethnicity and more focused on welfare policy.

In general, the political debate over welfare during this period undergirded a greater acceptance of public relief programs and supported their enlarged enrollment. Boston's Depression mayors, all Irish Democrats, supported the enlarged expenditures of the public welfare department during this decade, each appropriating a larger percentage of the city's budget to fund its operations. Even the most conservative of these Democrats, Frederick Mansfield, insisted that "the city will give as liberal aid as possible to all worthy welfare recipients," adding that he realized the "social importance" of the city's "obligations" to the needy.[21]

The majority of City Council members also expressed support for the city's attempt to aid those in need. Several of them referred to relief as the "first duty of the city." Likewise, they often suggested that people in need were "entitled" to public aid and that stigma no longer be associated with it. They demanded that the welfare department increase its grants to families, make the application process easier, and decrease the work requirements. As during the 1920s, the ethnic politicians on the City Council advanced a more democratic vision of welfare, insisting that as elected officials, they had a duty to participate in welfare policy and a right to knowledge about particular cases. Accordingly, City Council president Joseph McGrath exhorted his colleagues in 1932: "I say to every member of the Council, you were elected to take care of the people of your district. . . . When worthy cases are brought to your attention, it is your duty to do what you can, your sworn duty, and don't you get scared from doing it."[22]

However, even as city politicians appropriated unprecedented sums for the city's poor relief programs, new criticism of welfare emerged and new issues entered the welfare debate during the 1930s. Welfare fraud, the relationship between employment and welfare, and the role of the federal government became troubling topics in the local political debate over welfare. The conflicts over these issues reflected divisions among Irish politicians and between the Irish and other ethnic groups. Less a conflict over whether public aid should be provided, the political debate in the 1930s concerned who would receive and who would administer public welfare benefits.

The fear of fraud and corruption had long been part of the debate over poor relief. As urbanization and immigration changed social relations in the late nineteenth century, concerns about fraud and corruption intensified. Efforts, successful in New York City and Philadelphia, to dismantle municipal poor relief programs as well as the campaign against Civil War pensions embodied these sentiments. The representatives of Boston's Protestant charities and many of the city's native-born Republican leaders had long expressed concern about the potential of relief to encourage fraud among recipients and corruption among public officials. Close supervision and small grants, they argued, could prevent abuses of poor relief. Boston's Jewish and Catholic charity leaders had always expressed less concern about the potential for fraud and corruption related to relief. Likewise, the city's ethnic politicians, rather than criticizing poor relief for its potential to corrupt, had, instead, criticized the "guards" against fraud—close supervision of recipients and small grants.[23]

With the enlargement of welfare expenditures during the early thirties, the political discussion turned again to welfare fraud. Unlike in the earlier debates, however, ethnic politicians joined in the concern over welfare fraud. Both on the floor of the City Council and in the newspapers, accusations of welfare fraud were lodged both against "fakers," people who were supposedly receiving public aid even though they did not need it, and against the welfare department. "I say that the relief rolls of this city are padded, and I want to see the thing cleaned up," charged Councilman John I. Fitzgerald, representative of a congested area downtown and critic of Mayor Curley. That same year, Councilman Joseph McGrath, representing a section of Dorchester, challenged the public welfare department to "give us an honest deal, and to get rid of the fakers." The councilmen argued that the "fakers" posed a threat both to families who "deserved" aid and to the "honest" homeowner.[24]

Even though the councilmen's complaints resembled criticisms by native-born Republican politicians of the enlarged welfare expenditures in the 1920s, they were different. The debate during the previous decade had been one of expansion versus constraints. The concern over welfare fraud during the 1930s was not over uniform expansion but over who would receive the benefits. As Councilman McGrath put it: "I have no objection at all . . . to every single worthy family getting all the assistance the city can afford . . . [but] if there is one man or one old person in one of the rooming-houses of our city, or in any ward of the city, who is being denied the proper assistance that we are paying for because some family that is not entitled to it is getting it . . . I want to know." In addition, during the debates of the 1920s, city councilmen had argued in favor of enlarged welfare expenditures, using the concept of entitlement, a radical departure from the traditional concept of poor relief being at the prerogative of the city's Overseers. By the 1930s, the city councilmen assumed the notion of entitlement to public support even as they demanded more discretion.[25]

As during the 1920s, the criticism led to numerous investigations of the welfare department and recipients. In the previous decade, however, the op-

ponents of welfare expansion were the primary instigators of special investigations; during the 1930s, the City Council's ethnic politicians as well as
Mayor Curley called for these special studies. The police conducted the most
notorious of these investigations in 1932. Criticized by most, this investigation involved local police officers calling on welfare recipients to verify their
need. The social work community and the Overseers condemned the use of
police officers, but the City Council members were divided, with some believing that local police might have a better knowledge of the families in
the neighborhood than the overextended visitors from the welfare department. Eventually, though, the council agreed that the police investigation
had "degenerated into a contest of mutual recrimination" between the welfare department and the police department, and the investigation was
abandoned.[26]

The failure of the police investigation, however, did not end further investigations of the welfare department and welfare recipients. Throughout
the 1930s, the City Council, the Finance Commission, the mayor's office, and
social work organizations investigated the workings of the welfare department. None of these studies turned up evidence of widespread fraud on the
part of either the personnel of the department or public aid recipients. The
investigations concluded, instead, that enormous demands put on the welfare department by the Depression had stretched the welfare department to
its limit and that administrative reform was needed.[27]

The numerous investigations of welfare programs set a tone of distrust
toward both the welfare department and recipients. Though always careful
to portray themselves as supportive of "deserving" welfare recipients, the
members of the council attacked the "undeserving" welfare recipients, calling them, as one member put it "a Frankenstein in this city." City councilmen reported stories of welfare recipients who owned expensive cars and
wore "fine clothing." The councilmen complained that welfare recipients
were running for office, one telling a story about a welfare recipient who
had supposedly spent $2,000 in a campaign for City Council, riding in a
"privately-owned seven-passenger automobile" in a political parade. Vow-
ing to confront the "unworthy" welfare recipients, Councilman McGrath
urged his fellow council members: "So let us stand up and fight until we have
on the run every fakir [sic] and crook who is getting from the city what he is
not properly entitled to. Let us have the intestinal fortitude now that we have
started and are getting them on the run, to go through to the very end."[28]

With each investigation of welfare recipients and accusation of fraud by city councilmen, the city's welfare program lost credibility and respect. In the process, welfare recipients were described as monsters and criminals that drained the city of resources. Because the city councilmen personalized their attacks on people who they felt were "unjustly on the welfare," their comments were harsher, in many ways, than earlier attacks on the welfare system.[29]

The relationship between work and welfare also divided politicians as they debated the value of work relief programs during the 1930s. Even before the introduction of federal work relief programs, Mayor Curley had championed a public works program for the unemployed. He insisted that "men" wanted work, not a dole, adding that the outright grant "saps initiative, and makes of a man a chronic loafer." Curley argued that work relief, unlike direct relief, preserved people's dignity and respect, stressing that "dependency" was particularly debilitating for men. Two decades earlier, Curley had argued that the unemployed needed to depend on public aid much as widows with children did. But now that he, as well as many constituents, were more solidly middle-class, he adopted the rhetoric of independence for wage-earning men.[30]

Curley opponents—Yankee and ethnic alike—questioned Curley's motives for wanting to enlarge the city's public works program, and they blocked his efforts to create a public employment program. Nevertheless, they shared his views on the need to "separate" unemployed men from traditional relief recipients. As a result, local welfare offices set up separate programs and requirements for the unemployed to spare them the embarrassment of being "on the welfare." The jobless did not face the same level of investigation and supervision as other relief cases, and the department did not require the unemployed to provide extensive family information when they applied for aid. Federal relief programs made similar distinctions as they set up programs for the unemployed.[31]

The design and hiring guidelines of both local and federal work programs gave preference to—and, in some cases, restricted work relief assignments to—male "breadwinners with two or more dependents." Work projects open to women were in fields segregated by gender and valued less. More by local practice than design, the federal work projects also discriminated along ethnic and racial lines, and Irish-Americans benefited the most from the federal work programs. While the discrimination did not go unnoticed, it went largely unchecked. Boston's Urban League and local NAACP chapter protested the exclusion of African-Americans from work projects and questioned the placement of black women in domestic service positions. Their criticism exposed the racial and gender inequity of the New Deal work programs, but, even more important, it represented an engagement by black leaders in the politics of public welfare. Concessions were made to the city's black organizations, but fair inclusion was hardly achieved. The scope of the work projects continued to be limited by availability of funds and by persistent patterns of discrimination. The result was the popular perception that the programs were based more on politics than on need. In reality, while the federal work programs limited the individualized politics of urban patronage, they reinforced the larger gender and racial politics when determining who should be included and how in federally funded work projects.[32]

The bitterness over access to federal funds was also sharpened by the fact that Boston did not benefit much from the earliest New Deal work relief programs, the Civil Works Administration (CWA) and the first Federal Emergency Relief Administration (FERA). With its comparatively extensive public and private relief programs, Boston did not face the crisis of other urban centers, and federal money was directed elsewhere. Moreover, the state's Republican leadership was slow to compete for federal assistance. Boston's chances for special attention diminished further when Mayor Curley's initial support for Roosevelt soured. Neither Harold Ikes nor Harry Hopkins, the directors of Roosevelt's federal work relief programs, trusted Curley, and they approved few of his proposals. With the mayoral election of Frederick Mansfield, a conservative Irish Democrat, and the establishment of the second FERA in 1934, Boston began to get a larger share of federal work relief funds, and a greater level of inclusion was demonstrated locally. But even the second wave of work relief did not stem the growing requests for public aid.[33]

As it became clear that these federal work relief programs were not significantly reducing the public relief rolls, political disputes intensified. Some on the City Council criticized any attempt to use work relief programs as a means of reducing the city's relief rolls. Work relief, they argued, should go to those who had managed to keep themselves off welfare. Others, however, wanted to know why the infusion of federal work relief funding had not helped reduce the outlays by the public welfare department. The more conservative members of the City Council wanted to be sure that the welfare department was not supporting anyone who might be "employable." Henry Lee Shattuck, the council's token Brahmin member, led this effort, but some ethnic politicians, including Mayor Mansfield, joined it.[34]

The disputes over unemployment assistance and work programs significantly affected welfare policy. First, by demanding that the unemployed be kept separate from traditional poor relief, the City Council members reinforced the stigma of direct relief. Second, by creating categories such as "employable," they cast other welfare recipients—the elderly, mothers with dependent children, the ill and the handicapped—as "unemployable." Third, the focus on the unemployed overshadowed the other categorical aid programs that became the larger part of the welfare budget by the end of the 1930s. Taken together, these developments created inequalities—in terms of funding and administration—among the city's various relief programs. Most significantly, though, these developments sharpened the distinctions between unemployment relief—a program in most regards for men—and relief programs for other needy people—women, children, and the elderly.

While thousands in Boston relied on the federal work programs of the FERA and the WPA, an uneasy relationship existed between local politics and the new federal welfare programs. With Curley as mayor in the early thirties, Boston was regularly passed over for special federal assistance; and, although more federal moneys came to Boston during the administrations of Frederick Mansfield (1934–38) and Maurice Tobin (1938–46), there remained a strong sentiment that Boston was not getting its fair share of federal aid. The City Council's more critical members, Clement Norton and Shattuck, complained the loudest that the city was not making enough of an effort to secure federal money and often provided information to the council that suggested that Boston was receiving less than other large cities. Councilman John Dowd, hardly a political ally of either Norton or Shattuck, agreed: "I don't know what Boston has done to the Federal authorities, but it would appear to me from the attitude of the E.R.A., P.W.A. and all the other alphabets of the Federal Government that the City of Boston is being given the best kidding to be found anywhere throughout the country." Dowd, a populist defender of the poor, saw the lack of federal money as proof that the people who applied for these programs stood little chance of either gaining employment or receiving an adequate number of hours in work relief to support their families. The criticisms of the federal government voiced on the floor of the City Council were part of the local resistance to federal intervention that historian Charles H. Trout has traced in his study of the city during the thirties. But the complaints of the councilmen were as much over the workings of welfare, debated long before the entrance of the federal government, as they were over federal intervention.[35]

Changes in Public Welfare

Even as the political debate over welfare continued, public welfare underwent important changes during this period. The expenditures on public welfare rose from nearly $2.5 million in 1929 to nearly $12.9 million in 1939, a fivefold increase. Likewise, the department's caseload nearly quintupled, from 7,319 in 1929 to 34,604 in 1939 while the city's population decreased. To handle the increased demand for services, the department's personnel expanded to over five hundred employees by the end of the decade, far more than the fifty employees who worked for the department in 1929. As the department grew, the Overseers of the Public Welfare became the most important city department for the expenditures of revenue. Because the state legislature controlled the city's debt limit and restricted its power to tax, the increased welfare expenditures represented a shift in the priorities of the city's spending. To meet the demands of the welfare budget, the city reduced its payroll in other departments, cutting its workforce nearly in half between 1933 and 1940. The employees who remained faced periodic furloughs, reduced hours, and wage cuts. The city also cut back on its public works budget. By 1940, the welfare department received 17.9 cents of every tax dollar, a fivefold increase over the 1929 allocation.[36]

The expansion of public welfare, however, was not the only dramatic change in the city's public aid program during the 1930s. The categories of people aided changed dramatically as well. With the crisis of the Depression, the city's public welfare rolls swelled with the unemployed, and unlike during the 1920s, public officials openly acknowledged the public assistance provided for these men. Identifying unemployment as a "new" category of public aid, the Finance Commission wrote in 1932: "To the two forms of relief granted by the department for the past several years, and, therefore, well known to the people generally, mothers' aid and dependent aid, a new type has been added as a result of the industrial depression—unemployment relief." Members of the City Council, moreover, defended the use of public welfare by the unemployed. As Councilman Israel Ruby put it: "Today if a person is on the level and cannot get a job, it is no longer considered a disgrace, pauperism, or shameful for him to resort to public welfare in order to protect his family." Mayor Curley and members of the City Council, likewise, identified the "unemployment relief" as the primary reason for the public welfare department's increased costs, and during the first half of the decade, their assessment was correct. In 1929, 26 percent of the Dependent

Aid cases represented unemployed people or families; by 1933, 76 percent did. The unemployed far outnumbered other public welfare recipients, and the plight of these men became the focus of the political debate over welfare. It also prompted the renaming of the Dependent Aid program as General Relief. Male breadwinners, even unemployed ones, were not to be considered dependents.[37]

While expansion in unemployment aid dominated the first half of the decade and set the tone of the political debate, "categorical aid" to the elderly and dependent children became an increasingly larger share of the public welfare budget after 1935. This shift actually began in 1932, when Dependent Aid expenditures began to drop as work relief programs were introduced to Boston. It became most noticeable, however, after the 1935 passage of the Social Security Act that included Old Age Assistance (OAA) and Aid to Dependent Children (ADC). Federal funding for OAA and ADC as well as more-liberal federal guidelines began an expansion of these categorical relief programs that would eventually outstrip spending for General Relief.[38]

OAA and ADC followed somewhat different paths during the 1930s, not only because of the different origins of these programs, but also because of their different recipient pools and the politics surrounding these programs. The Massachusetts Old Age Assistance program predated the Social Security Act. Passed in 1930, OAA was the product of over two decades of agitation for a public aid program for the state's elderly. The campaign for OAA had included proposals for various programs for the elderly, some contributory and others noncontributory, some universal and some limited to citizens. Its strongest supporters were working-class men's organizations, such as the Massachusetts branch of the American Federation of Labor and the Fraternal Order of Eagles.[39]

Proposals for a publicly funded old age program met staunch criticism from the leaders of the Protestant private charities and the state's Board of Charity. As a result, the legislation that finally established OAA, much like the Mothers' Aid program in Massachusetts, was a fairly conservative welfare measure. In essence, it was a needs-based relief program administered by the public welfare department. It was envisioned as a limited public relief program available to citizens older than 70 who did not have family to support them and who had lived in the commonwealth for at least twenty years. Even though the legislation mandated that the aid be "sufficient to provide suitable and dignified care," it did not set a mandatory level of support nor did it specify guidelines for eligibility.[40]

The popular demand for this program, along with its passage coinciding with the onset of the Depression, resulted in rapid and significant enrollment in the program. In response, the state Department of Public Welfare endeavored to limit its expansion. Francis Bardwell, a leader among the Protestant charities, headed up the new Old Age Division, and he campaigned to have localities present the program not as a pension but as an assistance program. "The fact that this law had early been branded as 'old age pension' had to be met and the difference between a pension and assistance explained," he wrote in 1931. "While a pension is based on an individual's legal right, this law [for Old Age Assistance] is based upon a person's need." When enrollment in the program doubled the first year, Bardwell tried to limit enrollment and expenses by tightening eligibility requirements and lowering the grant size.[41]

Despite efforts by the state Department of Public Welfare to curtail the growth of OAA, popular and political support for this program led to its liberalization and expansion. With the election of Curley as governor in 1934, Walter V. McCarthy, who had heralded the enlargement of Boston's public welfare department in the twenties, replaced Richard Conant as state commissioner of public welfare. The Protestant social work network, of which Conant was a prominent member, demurred, but those objections were ignored. Under McCarthy's direction, the state's OAA program was liberalized and expanded. Although the department continued to consider personal behavior as an important criterion of eligibility (or "deservedness"), it loosened its standards. During the program's early years, the state board stipulated that the OAA was only for "deserving citizens" and recommended that all "deserters, nonsupporters, confirmed alcoholics, drug-addicts, and chronic offenders against the law" be excluded. Beginning in the mid-thirties, however, the board took a more liberal approach to eligibility, contending that it was a person's "present behavior, not the past that determines whether someone [was] deserving" and concluding: "If there is a question whether the applicant is deserving, he should be given the benefit of the doubt." The board raised property levels so that more homeowners could qualify for the program, and it assured families that they would not be held responsible for the support of elderly relatives who might qualify for the program.[42]

OAA also enjoyed local political support. OAA was a popular program, funded in part with state money. Members of the Boston City Council complained about the treatment "old folks" received when they applied for aid, and demanded that they be treated differently from other applicants. In their descriptions of the poor, the councilmen depicted the elderly as "worthy unfortunates" who had worked hard throughout their lives. Unlike in their discussions of public welfare in general, they seldom connected increases in OAA with fraud or corruption. Appropriations for OAA regularly passed the City Council without question.[43]

Even though OAA was available to both men and women who qualified, the program was understood and discussed in terms of support for elderly men. Growing out of campaigns for old age pensions, the Old Age Assistance program was primarily a concession that allowed a larger number of elderly men to receive outdoor relief. The program's focus on men could be seen at the state level when, immediately after its passage, the state board hired forty visitors—all men—to oversee the program. Unlike the much smaller and all female Mothers' Aid staff, the visitors for the OAA were not expected to supervise OAA recipients. Instead, the visitors oversaw the "general welfare" of these cases, relying on voluntary visits by the elderly clients' clergy or family for specific information.[44]

During the 1930s, the popular and political support for OAA cast this program as a "good" welfare program. Beginning in 1934, OAA saw greater annual increases in both caseload and expenditures than both Dependent Aid and Mothers' Aid. The transfer of elderly cases out of the Dependent Aid category into the Old Age category explains this in part, but much of the growth in OAA was a result of enrollment in the program by people not previously on public aid and of increases in the grants given each case. During the first year, the average grant to recipients of OAA was approximately $5 a week, but these grants saw a steady increase during the 1930s, taking a sharp jump in 1937, when Massachusetts set a minimum payment of $30 per month, to take full advantage of federal reimbursement.[45]

The other categorical aid program, Mothers' Aid, followed a different course during the 1930s. With the political focus on male unemployment and aid to the elderly, the effects of the Depression on Mothers' Aid recipients and on other mothers with dependent children went little noticed or discussed. Throughout the 1920s the Mothers' Aid program had lost ground, and its appropriations from both the state and the city of Boston had leveled off. After reaching a peak in 1919, the number of annual cases had leveled off as well. The strong support that the Mothers' Aid program had enjoyed at its passage had waned during the more conservative decade of the 1920s. Political attention had turned to campaigns for an old age pension and to the needs of the chronically unemployed, issues which concerned women both directly and indirectly but which were largely cast as problems faced by men.[46]

With the onset of the Depression, however, the Mothers' Aid caseload in Boston and statewide began to increase. Elizabeth Moloney, state supervisor of Mothers' Aid, defended these increases and related them to the general unemployment crisis. Never a grant of full support, Mothers' Aid supposedly made up the difference between family income and family needs. Moloney argued that Mothers' Aid families saw their other incomes decrease as a result of the unemployment of older children in the family and the difficulty of mothers finding part-time work, a practice Moloney had initially not stressed but that became increasingly necessary to support the family. In addition, the Depression made it difficult for the children who reached the working age of sixteen to find work and, thus, they tended to remain dependent on the family income. Moreover, the Depression had curtailed aid to these families from relatives and from private charitable organizations.[47]

Moloney's defense of the increases in the Mothers' Aid program during the 1930s was not matched in the political arena, however, and appropriations for the program failed to keep up with the increase in caseload. As appropriations lagged, individual grants were cut. Throughout the history of Mothers' Aid in Massachusetts, the commonwealth had led other states in the size of grants it provided to families that qualified for Mothers' Aid, and grants in Boston usually exceeded what was calculated as "adequate" for an urban family ($60 a month in 1932). The program was able to do so by restricting the number of cases and, during the 1920s, even reducing the number of cases. During the Depression, that policy became less feasible, and so grant size began to be reduced and time limits imposed. At the state level, Moloney complained about the reduction in grant sizes. "For twenty years the State Department of Public Welfare has labored to raise the level of relief to mothers with dependent children from pitifully small doses of relief in kind to adequate cash relief," she wrote in her 1932 report. She argued that children would be hurt by the cuts, and she particularly opposed across-the-board cuts since they undermined the casework policy of the program.[48]

Pressured by the crisis of the Depression and insufficient appropriations for Mothers' Aid, Moloney took a more restrictive view toward Mothers'

Aid than she had earlier. She criticized localities for enrolling as many families as possible in this program, accusing them of doing so in order to receive state reimbursement. She especially deplored the inclusion of unemployed families in Mothers' Aid, insisting that Mothers' Aid be restricted to
mothers with dependent children or to families with totally incapacitated
male heads of household. In defense of her program, Moloney turned on
the unemployed, saying, "A man who is lazy rather than sick should be
forced to work."[49]

Moloney also complained about the increasing practice by localities, including Boston, to enroll more "non-widow" families, meaning families
with mothers who had been divorced, deserted, separated, or never married,
as well as families with fathers who were unable to support their families because of disability, illness, or incarceration. During the twenties, Moloney
had displayed a less judgmental approach, but with funds tight and localities
looking for ways to aid families affected by the Depression, she became more
guarded about the program's use: "Hither to Mothers' Aid has been granted
only to the best type of mothers, but recently, in order to secure reimbursement from the Commonwealth, some local boards are extending Mothers'
Aid to any mother who may possibly come within the law. Fitness of the
mother and her maintenance of good standards of home and child care must
still be insisted upon." By using the "fitness" measures of the Mothers' Aid
program to complain about the "raiding" of Mothers' Aid funds by local
welfare departments, Moloney was joining the divisive debate over welfare
funding that assumed entitlement while maintaining distinctions.[50]

The introduction of the federal Aid to Dependent Children program
(ADC) in 1935 rescued and reinvigorated the Massachusetts Mothers' Aid
program even as it shifted the focus from the mother to the dependent children. With the prospect of federal funding, Moloney became less defensive
about the inclusion of more "non-widows" in the program. The shift in the
focus away from funding mothers and toward funding dependent children
pleased Moloney, who saw the new program as a better guarantee of support
for poor children. The availability of federal funds for this program, along
with Moloney's less defensive posture about an increase in local enroll-
ments, resulted in a significant increase in both cases and expenditures at the
local level. Boston's ADC cases jumped from 2,570 in 1937 to 4,018 in 1939,
and its expenditures went up 80 percent. Given the employment crisis of
the 1930s, ADC cases were categorized as "unemployable," a status that Moloney, who had never been an advocate of wage work for Mothers' Aid recipients, did not oppose.[51]

The prolonged Depression, along with the introduction of federally funded programs for the elderly poor and dependent children, meant that Boston's relief expenditures remained well above their 1929 level as the thirties drew to a close. Even though federal work relief programs had reduced the outlays on Dependent Aid from their 1932 high, expenditures on this program had increased 418 percent between 1929 and 1939, and there was no indication that these costs would return to pre-Depression levels. Added to these increased expenditures on Dependent Aid was the cost of categorical aid to the elderly poor and dependent children, both of which had increased over 200 percent during the 1930s.[52]

The political response to persistent public welfare expenditures was mixed. As it became clear that federal assistance had not reduced local costs, critics called for welfare reform. Describing the city's relief expenditures as a "semi-permanent problem," Henry Lee Shattuck and his associates at a newly established watchdog organization, the Municipal Research Bureau, complained: "Some form of welfare aid is now available for virtually every type of personal misfortune without regard for duration." They argued for increased federal and state reimbursement for Dependent Aid and a clearer definition of relief programs for the "employable" and "unemployable." Maurice Tobin, the conservative Democratic mayor elected in 1937, echoed these fiscally constrained sentiments and began cutting city expenditures on relief. No significant local political debate over welfare policy unfolded, however, as the decade came to a close. With the introduction of the state-administered unemployment insurance program in 1938, Boston's City Council members stopped discussing municipal relief in connection with "employable" men and, in the process, shifted their attention away from the issue of public relief. Aid to Dependent Children and Old Age Assistance, perceived as programs for needy children and the elderly, came under little political fire despite their enlargement toward the end of the decade. The federal oversight and reimbursement of these categorical aid programs further weakened the local political debate over welfare policy, ending two decades of political disputes and discussions about municipal relief.[53]

In the years following the Depression, Boston's public welfare program maintained its function as the primary source of financial assistance to the city's needy; however, it also remained a fragmented program seldom adequate to meet the needs of the poor. A patchwork of distinct programs, public welfare remained sensitive to changing political and social trends. As federal work programs, the new Unemployment Insurance program, and the war economy took unemployed men off the welfare rolls, General Relief

once again became a poorly funded program that aided primarily the destitute and the sick. Locally funded, this program offered support that was far
from adequate for its recipients. In contrast, Old Age Assistance and Aid to
Dependent Children continued to expand. Federal and state funding limited
the local cost of these programs. This encouraged not only the growth of
these categorical aid programs but also a loosening of their eligibility requirements as localities sought to transfer recipients from the locally funded
General Relief program to OAA and ADC to qualify for reimbursement. In
the 1940s the Massachusetts ADC program loosened the "fit home" stipulation, allowing the inclusion of children of unmarried women. Likewise there
was pressure from cities and town officials to drop the citizenship requirement for OAA. Neither stipulation was mandated federally but neither were
they prevented under federal guidelines. Localities saw these changes as a
means to collect federal and state funds for cases they might otherwise be
expected to bear alone. Even with the higher level of aid required by these
programs, localities recognized them as fiscally advantageous, since the requirement of "adequate support" was seldom met in practice.

ADC's association with widows was severed with the creation of survivors
insurance in 1939. Part of the amendments to the Social Security Act, survivors insurance aided mothers whose deceased husbands qualified for Social Security. An attempt to spend the larger than expected surplus in the
Social Security trust fund, survivors insurance departed from the notion
of Social Security as a contributory program. Its support of families, however, met no political opposition. Survivors insurance began the removal of
children of widows from the ADC program and the transformation of ADC
into a program for poor but less entitled children.[54]

Political changes at the state level in the late 1930s prompted new calls for
welfare reform. Following the election of Republican Leverett Saltonstall as
governor in 1938, Arthur G. Rotch replaced Walter McCarthy as commissioner of public welfare. Rotch, a leader in the Council of Social Agencies
and member of the Protestant social work network in Boston, attempted to
reduce the increasing cost of public welfare through administrative reform.
To reduce costs and, in theory, to end the "inequality" among public welfare
programs, Rotch dismantled the state's separate Old Age, Aid to Dependent
Children, and General Relief departments, returning the administration of
all relief programs to the local level. The state visitors were assigned to new
district offices, where they focused on the training and oversight of local welfare offices. State visitors discontinued casework, returning all field work to

local welfare officials. This reform returned public welfare to the localities, ending a two-decade trend toward centralized administration.[55]

As with earlier attempts to rein in welfare expansion, Republican welfare reform had little effect in limiting the fiscal expansion of public assistance, particularly in Boston, but these reforms had significant consequences both in the short and long term. By returning welfare programs to local administration, the reforms fostered even greater distinctions among Boston's public welfare programs. Not only did grant levels remain uneven among these programs, but services also differed. By the late 1940s, Boston's General Relief recipients were receiving little or no aid beyond the most limited financial assistance. The job placement efforts enacted during the Depression were discontinued, along with the local food and fuel distribution to these cases. As the relief and jobs programs of the thirties came to an end, public aid became, once again, a meager source of support with only somewhat less social stigma than before the Depression. OAA and ADC—programs that, by design, intended to guarantee more than financial assistance—offered some services, but the type and level of services provided by these programs differed. Boston's OAA recipients received significantly better service from the city's public welfare office than ADC cases did, including regular visits, better medical attention, and an easier appeal procedure. ADC families—in almost every case mothers with dependent children—received less attention, fewer services, and limited information about the appeals process. Whereas the department interpreted eligibility for OAA quite liberally, it maintained a strict interpretation of the qualifications for ADC. Even as the state moved to liberalize the program, the Boston welfare office continued to use the "fit home" requirement to exclude children of unmarried mothers. In some cases, according to one report, the department used the "fit home" requirement to "punish" unmarried mothers by forcing these cases to remain on the less generous General Relief program indefinitely, after which they would be enrolled as ADC recipients. The differences in levels of funding and types of services among Boston's public assistance program reflected the historical development of these welfare programs as well as pervasive ideas about the entitlement of different groups.[56]

Even as demarcations among public aid programs persisted, the long-run consequence of the welfare reforms of the late 1930s was a merging of all public assistance programs in popular and political perception. By abolishing the state's ADC and OAA departments and consolidating all relief programs, these reforms assured that these categorical relief programs would become administratively and politically attached to general poor relief and that their legislative association with old age and unemployment insurance would be forgotten. OAA and ADC had earlier been proposed as "wedges" toward more adequate and less stigmatized social provisions. As the Depression ended, OAA and ADC, along with General Relief, became "welfare" as we still know it today—stigmatized public assistance for the poor.

CONCLUSION

Placing Boston in Social Policy Theories

THAT WELFARE programs in America are fragmented and limited is a common observation. While other rich industrial nations developed centralized programs of workers' compensation, old age pensions, health insurance, unemployment insurance, and family allowances during the twentieth century, the United States crafted far less universal programs and implemented them at both the state and the federal level. Moreover, a commitment to private means of assuring these social provisions persisted, most notably in the absence of a state-sponsored health insurance program but characteristic, in fact, of all the programs of social provisions established during the twentieth century. The limit of provision was "adequate support," either means-tested or keyed to previous wage force participation. The result has been a semi-welfare state, in terms of the scope, universality, and operation of public welfare provisions. The implementation of such partial programs of social provision and the linking of those programs to private sector and market efforts have narrowed the meaning of the word "welfare" to means-tested public assistance. Rather than suggesting the well-being of all, welfare in the United States is the care and support of the unfortunate poor.

What explains the creation of this semi-welfare state? The traditional explanation for the United States' limited welfare state was that Americans, more than the citizens of other industrialized nations, were strongly wed to liberal notions of individual responsibility and opportunity. Ironically, this theory of limited ideological support for state enlargement came into prominence in the immediate postwar period, a period marked by tremendous growth of the state apparatus, including the expansion of the landmark social provision programs passed during the New Deal. Both critics and advocates of American liberalism helped solidify American exceptionalism during an intense Cold War. They stressed America's intellectual disinclination for public provisions even as the enlargement of New Deal programs was coupled with the introduction of new programs of social provision during the 1960s, most significantly Medicare in 1965.

The 1970s and 1980s brought to an end the postwar growth in social welfare programs. The cooling of the postwar economy, the weakening of the political consensus for governmental growth, and the sharpening of social tensions around race, gender, and ethnicity blocked further enlargement and, in fact, prompted the scaling back of some programs. The politics and economics of the later postwar period which began to take shape during the Reagan years demanded further retreat from government-provided social supports. Although the new global economy and the end of the Cold War prompted unprecedented economic growth in the United States, governmental social provisions were disparaged, even identified as the cause of the economic downturn of the 1970s. Popular and political disdain for governmental programs of social provisions was only intensified when many industrialized nations that had made a commitment to a welfare state began to reassess their commitment to cradle-to-grave social supports.[1]

In this context scholars began again to consider the peculiarities of the social support programs in the United States. The liberal values interpretation no longer seemed adequate. Not only did the expansion of governmental function in the postwar period contradict the idea of an American commitment to classic liberal tenets, but, upon reconsideration, so did much of American history. Far from taking a laissez-faire stance, the government at all levels had regularly intervened in the American economy and society, whether by subsidizing railroad development or determining racial and gender relations through legal codes. Looking through the revisionist lens, scholars of social welfare resurrected the history of Civil War pensions as an example of early federal provision and saw in Progressive-era reforms the making of a centralized system of social provisions. The new approach dismissed not only home-grown claims of American liberalism but also theories about the liberal bent of American statecraft advanced by scholars beyond the United States.[2]

Debunking the myth of American faithfulness to classic liberalism proved easier than explaining the peculiar history and composition of social policy in this country. An examination of institutional politics was one tack to explain the semi-welfare state in the United States. This approach contended that the federalism of the U.S. political system along with the comparatively unique phenomenon of universal suffrage for all free men—all of whom enjoyed at least the possibility of patronage—siphoned off potential demands for centralized social provision. The civil service reforms of the late nineteenth century did little to curb patronage or to create administrative structures adequate to implement widespread social programs. Progressive-era experiments in social provisions did not enjoy widespread support or implementation, excepting the maternalistic schemes such as mothers' pensions and female labor regulation that used gender as a tool to assure, in theory at least, universality of need and benefit. Not until the crisis of the Great Depression and the political strength of the Roosevelt administration, which forged a "reform regime" with cross-class support, did the United States begin to implement widespread public social welfare measures. The "boldness" of the New Deal reform regime, however, was constrained by institutional politics, including the lack of true democracy in the South and from the implementation of New Deal reforms at both federal and state levels. These constraints not only weakened welfare state development but also divided the citizenry with some, primarily white men, enjoying better welfare provisions and guarantees than others, often women and people of color. The result of these institutional constraints was a welfare system with limited political or social strength.[3]

Attention to social relations provided another means to explain the unique history of American social provisions. The legacy of racism in this country and its impact on policy formation resulted in the exclusion of most people of color from the programs of social provision emerging during the early twentieth century. This exclusion was both overt, in the denial of aid that should have been available, and covert, by the design of programs for which most people of color did not qualify. The role of women in social welfare history—a role that seems more pronounced in the United States than elsewhere—and the efforts by women to address the needs of poor women and children also demanded attention. Female welfare advocates pressed for the enlargement of welfare programs, but their proposals included hefty doses of supervision in exchange for financial support that, compared with traditional poor aid, was more generous but, in terms of adequacy, remained limited. Moreover, the maternal welfare effort contributed to a normalizing of an idealized nuclear family with a male breadwinner with dependent wife and children. The class specificity of the nuclear family ideal and the de facto exclusion of most people of color, many of whom faced barriers to incomes sufficient to realize the single wage ideal, suggested that gender ideals often connote racial identities. Focusing on race and gender has exposed how the organization of social relations within our democratic system, and not only the limits of our institutions themselves, affects the characteristics of our welfare provisions.[4]

Coming full circle, ideas are once again being examined to explain our welfare history. While this path can merely retread earlier mythologies of individualism, a thoughtful reconsideration of American values to explain the development of social policy in the United States seems appropriate. Careful to cast values not only in terms of what people hold dear but also as national memory, real and mythologized, historian Alice Kessler-Harris urges us to consider the power of the idealized family to constrain policy formation. Schemes of social provisions during the Progressive era—and more so during the New Deal—were organized around notions of male breadwinning and female dependence even when, technically, the plans provided universal benefits. Kessler-Harris asks us to consider the way the ideal of family independence, including dependency within the family, explains the fragmentation of social welfare provisions in this country. Powerful ideas, as much as political structures and social relations, influenced social policy in the United States.[5]

The history of welfare politics in Boston resonates with these theories about American policy formation. Without question, the city's welfare history affirms the influence of formal political institutions on policy formation. The political structures in Boston were integrally related to, and partly determined, the level and type of democratic representation. During the nineteenth century, political accommodation allowed the inclusion of all men in formal politics even as it assured the continued influence of white native-born Bostonians and perpetuated traditions that limited public provisions to the poor. A challenge from without and a challenge from within reconstructed politics in Boston. Working outside the formal political system, women made new demands on the state with the proposal for a widows' pension. This campaign, along with other reform efforts by disenfranchised women, destabilized Boston's deferential and accommodationist politics. Their efforts did not transform city politics or even assure women's full political inclusion—something assured only by the federal amendment of 1920—but their agitation for influence and their demands for greater public responsibility for poor women and children ignited demands for better provisions for all poor families. These efforts also created an opening for political enlargement. Using the rhetoric of Progressive reform, ethnic immigrants, particularly the Irish but also Jews and later Italians, began to exert greater political influence and thus gained benefits for their own constituents, despite Progressive-era charter reforms that aimed to limit democratic influence. Thus, women's activism from outside the political system precipitated political change, but "ethnic progressivism" inside the political system transformed Boston's politics.[6]

As part of that political transformation, the public welfare department was forced to become more inclusive and responsive to poor families, and stigma for public aid lessened. A larger proportion of the city budget was devoted to social provisions for the needy, and the operations of the welfare department were debated in the formal political arena. The confrontational and populist language of inclusion offered very little to black Bostonians, who continued to be politically marginalized, but its rhetoric of inclusion set the stage for demands for political inclusion, hinted at in the 1930s but not influential until the civil rights era. The lack of political unity among ethnic Bostonians during the early twentieth century, however, limited the remaking of political institutions and the crafting of comprehensive social policy. As a result, public provisions to the poor were democratized, enlarged, and at least rhetorically transformed into a social right, but the conflictual social setting of this transformation led to a patchwork system of social provisions, implemented at the local, state, and national level.

Boston's welfare history pushes us beyond institutional interpretations, however, to consider the relationship of social relations to policy formation and the significance of ideas to outcome. The influx of large numbers of foreign immigrants in the late nineteenth century threatened and eventually reconstructed Boston's charity system. The sheer numbers of ethnic newcomers, most of whom were uneducated, poor, and employed in areas that assured only limited economic stability, demanded the enlargement of both private and public charity efforts. The growth of charity efforts, especially in the less accommodationist and more antagonistic political climate of city politics, aligned private efforts along religious identity—Catholic, Jewish, and Protestant—even as liberal Protestants sponsored nonsectarian private charity organizations. As the influence of Catholic and Jewish charities increased—a result of both their size and increasing political support—the differences between their orientation and the Protestant approach to caring for the poor became more pronounced. Protestant charities advanced liberal notions of individual responsibility and independence, even as they provided charity in instances when these values failed, as in the case of intemperance, or when these values could not be realized, as in old age. Catholic and Jewish charities took a distinctly less liberal approach to charity work, stressing instead collective responsibility and demonstrating a greater acceptance of dependence and human failing, without conflating the two. Catholic and Jewish charities did not emphasize wage work for poor mothers or the needy elderly, and they supported the creation of public welfare programs to aid these groups; meanwhile, Protestant organizations criticized the charities for encouraging dependency. Rejecting liberal Protestant promotion of independence and self-sufficiency, Catholic and Jewish charity leaders fueled an enlargement of social provisions and a lessening of the stigma associated with public support, a full decade before the crisis of the Depression promoted similar changes from the national level. As the social and political influence of Catholics and Jews increased, their conception of state responsibility increasingly came into conflict with liberal Protestant values.

The idealized male-headed, single-wage family proved a site of mediation and consensus for the Catholic, Jewish, and Protestant social visions. During the 1920s and especially in the 1930s, the tendency of Protestant liberalism to conceive of members of families as individuals was muted, and a vision of welfare based on family well-being came into focus. As both a site of dependency and an expression of market independence, the male-breadwinner family became the paramount blending of liberal ideals with conservative notions of family and sentimental affiliation. The crafting of social provisions toward this idealized family created a welfare system that, likewise, was an expression of liberal ideals and conservative social relations. The demand for and configuring of social welfare programs as support for idealized families enlarged the public commitment for social provisions, especially during the 1930s. At the same time, however, the emphasis on family welfare perpetuated the stigma of welfare for those outside male-headed families. Failure, not social responsibility, remained the impetus for social provisions to the poor, but rather than individualistic failing, which had been the focus in the nineteenth century, the emphasis now was on the failure of family.

The liberal/conservative basis of social provisions illustrated by Boston's welfare history prompts some reconsideration of the concept of "social citizenship." An idea advanced by British sociologist T. H. Marshall in 1949, social citizenship assured social rights that followed from civil and political rights. Eager to interpret efforts in Europe to create comprehensive welfare states and optimistic about the potential of welfare states to realize democracy fully, Marshall insisted that the promotion of social citizenship would not only lessen economic differences but also assure social unity. One might be tempted to see in the enlargement of social provisions in Boston the unfolding of Marshall's stages of democracy, for it is through the use of civil and political citizenship—formal and informal—that new demands on the state were made, first by women advancing widows' pensions and then by ethnic politicians lobbying for provisions for unemployed men with families. One could then conjecture that some failing in political structure or countervailing ideological forces—or both—somehow retarded or limited the realization of social citizenship.[7]

Better, I think, is to see the development of welfare programs for what they were, not what they should have been. In Boston, demands for state provisions were made and new functions were implemented. The social unity that advanced this enlargement, however, was not the consensus of individualized citizens—men and women—with social rights, but, instead, the unity prompted by the shared idealization of a male-headed, single-wage-earner family with social rights. For those who could not realize this idealized family formation, there were enlarged social provisions but provisions that neither ascribed nor engendered social citizenship. Some have called this a two-tier welfare system, but what Boston's social welfare history illuminates is that, although conflicted and weakened—structurally and ideologically—the programs of social provisions in the early twentieth century represented a political and social consensus about a family-based social citizenship. Celebrated by Marshall as an enlargement of rights from the political to the social sphere and touted as "urban liberalism" by American scholars, the expansion of welfare programs, premised as they were on family relations, did not assure economic citizenship for all individuals, even as they provided a wider safety net than had existed earlier. Moreover, the simultaneous linking of many welfare benefits to labor force participation sowed contradictions in family-based welfare policy that have grown as labor force opportunities for women and minorities have increased. Nevertheless, family-based social citizenship persists in policy considerations. Until a new consensus emerges, family-based social policy will continue to determine welfare programs, and social provisions for individual men, women, and children in need will continue to be fragmented and inadequate guarantees of full citizenship for all.[8]

NOTES

Preface

1. Gwendolyn Mink has been the most outspoken critic of social policy scholars; see "Aren't Poor Single Mothers Women? Feminists, Welfare Reform, and Welfare Justice," in *Whose Welfare?* (Ithaca: Cornell University Press, 1998), 171–88. Historical studies suggesting flaws and inequities in the welfare programs directed at poor mothers include: Gwendolyn Mink, *The Wages of Motherhood: Inequality in the Welfare State, 1917–1942* (Ithaca: Cornell University Press, 1995); Linda Gordon, *Pitied but Not Entitled: Single Mothers and the History of Welfare* (New York: The Free Press, 1994), and Joanne Goodwin, *Gender and the Politics of Welfare Reform: Mothers' Pensions in Chicago, 1911–1929* (Chicago: Chicago University Press, 1997).

2. An early claim of the success of welfare reform was "It's Working," *New Republic,* March 24, 1997. Since then welfare reform has drawn mixed reviews; see Diana M. Zuckerman, "The Evolution of Welfare Reform: Policy Changes and Current Knowledge," *Journal of Social Issues* 56 (winter 2000): 811–20. Critical overviews that take an historical perspective include: Michael B. Katz, *The Price of Citizenship: Redefining the American Welfare State* (New York: Metropolitan Books, 2001); Gwendolyn Mink, ed., *Welfare's End* (Ithaca: Cornell University Press, 1998); Eileen Boris, "When Work Is Slavery," in *Whose Welfare?,* 36–55; James T. Patterson, "'Reforming' Relief and Welfare: Thoughts on 1834 and 1996," in *With Us Always: A History of Private Charity and Public Welfare,* ed. Donald T. Critchlow and Charles H. Parker (New York: Rowman & Littlefield, 1998), 241–59; Joel F. Handler, *The Poverty of Welfare Reform* (New Haven: Yale University Press, 1995); and Linda Gordon, "Welfare Reform: A History Lesson," *Dissent* (summer 1994): 323–8.

Introduction. Placing Welfare History in Boston

1. "State-centered" analyses of American welfare policy include Ann Shola Orloff and Theda Skocpol, "Why Not Equal Protection?: Explaining the Politics of Public Social Spending in Britain, 1900–1911, and the United States, 1880s–1920," *American Sociological Review* 49 (1984): 726–50; Ann Shola Orloff, "The Political Origins of America's Belated Welfare State," in *The Politics of Social Policy in the United States,* ed. Margaret Weir, Ann

Shola Orloff, and Theda Skocpol (Princeton: Princeton University Press, 1988), 37–80; Theda Skocpol, *Protecting Soldiers and Mothers: The Political Origins of Social Policy in the United States* (Cambridge: Harvard University Press, 1992); Charles Noble, *Welfare as We Knew It: A Political History of the American Welfare State* (New York: Oxford University Press, 1997); and Edwin Amenta, *Bold Relief: Institutional Politics and the Origins of Modern American Social Policy* (Princeton: Princeton University Press, 1998).

2. Skocpol, the leading scholar among those advancing a political-institutional interpretation, makes passing reference to ethnic conflicts as a potential explanation for the differences between American and British welfare programs, but she dismisses ethnic conflicts as only reflecting struggles over political patronage; see *Protecting Soldiers and Mothers*, 272. In contrast, Clarke Chambers urges scholars of social welfare to pay more attention to ethnicity though few have; see "Toward a Redefinition of Welfare History," *Journal of American History* 73 (1986): 407–33. Matthew A. Crenson, in his history of the development of foster care, does consider religion's influence on state policy and argues, much as I do here, that the diversity of religious charities contributed to the fragmented nature of the American welfare system; see *Building the Invisible Orphanage: A Prehistory of the American Welfare State* (Cambridge: Harvard University Press, 1998). Scholars of Catholic history have also argued the important influence of religion on social welfare; see Kenneth J. Heineman, *A Catholic New Deal: Religion and Reform in Depression Pittsburgh* (University Park: Pennsylvania State University Press, 1999), and Dorothy M. Brown and Elizabeth McKeown, *The Poor Belong to Us: Catholic Charities and American Welfare* (Cambridge: Harvard University Press, 1997). Race has also been advanced as an important influence on American welfare provisions, an appropriate analysis given the disproportional use of public assistance by African Americans in the late twentieth century. The more salient observation about race and the early twentieth-century development of welfare, however, is the widespread exclusion of African Americans from public welfare programs and most private welfare programs. Only with federal welfare programs of the 1930s did the disproportionate level of poverty among African Americans begin to be addressed beyond the network of black churches and organizations. New Deal policies were often contradictory, sometimes including and other times excluding African American citizens. On race and welfare, see Amenta, *Bold Relief,* and Gwendolyn Mink, *The Wages of Motherhood: Inequality in the Welfare State, 1917–1943* (Ithaca: Cornell University Press, 1995).

3. Joanne Goodwin's study of the mothers' pension program in Chicago is an excellent example of the value of municipal studies of welfare policy. Goodwin argues that an unsettled debate over women's dependency, as well as local political struggles, undermined the implementation of mothers' aid in that city. She does not, however, discuss the ethnic and religious conflicts embedded in the political struggles over public welfare. See *Gender and the Politics of Welfare Reform: Mothers' Pensions in Chicago, 1911–1929* (Chicago: University of Chicago Press, 1997). For a selection of articles on gender and welfare in the U.S. context, see Linda Gordon, ed., *Women, the State, and Welfare* (Madi-

son: University of Wisconsin Press, 1990). Transnational studies of welfare programs using gender as a means of analysis include Ann Shola Orloff, "Gender and the Social Rights of Citizenship: The Comparative Analysis of Gender Relations and Welfare States," *American Sociological Review* 58 (June 1993): 303–28, and Seth Koven and Sonya Michel, "'Womanly Duties': Maternalist Politics and the Origins of Welfare States in France, Germany, Great Britain, and the United States, 1880–1920," *American Historical Review* 95 (1990): 1076–108. For examples of the "two-stream" argument, see Barbara Nelson, "The Origins of the Two-Channel Welfare State: Workmen's Compensation and Mothers' Aid," in Gordon, *Women, the State, and Welfare,* 123–51; Skocpol, *Protecting Soldiers and Mothers;* and Suzanne Mettler, *Dividing Citizens: Gender and Federalism in New Deal Public Policy* (Ithaca: Cornell University Press, 1998).

4. Commonwealth of Massachusetts, *Census of Massachusetts: 1910* (Boston, 1911). Historians have divided Boston's white native-born citizens into two groups: Yankees and Brahmins. Yankees, the majority of these Anglo-Americans, included skilled artisans, shopkeepers, tradesmen, and civil servants. Brahmins were a small and more elite group whose wealth was usually inherited from trade, fishing, finance, and manufacturing. Despite the difference in socioeconomic status, these groups often shared kinship networks. With the influx of immigration, the ties between Yankee and Brahmin Bostonians strengthened and the distinctions between them became less clear. Thus, for the purposes of this book, those white Protestant groups with long family ties to the city are identified as Yankee Bostonians. On ethnic groups in Boston, see John F. Stack Jr., *International Conflict in an American City: Boston's Irish, Italians, and Jews, 1935–1944* (Westport, Conn.: Greenwood Press, 1979), 20–4, and Oscar Handlin, *Boston's Immigrants: A Study in Acculturation* (New York: Athenaeum, 1970), 220. In 1875, the Massachusetts Census listed 2,389 Italians living in Boston (less than 1 percent of the population); in 1910, the number was 49,753 (7 percent). Between 1910 and 1920, the Italian population grew by another 27,000. In 1875, approximately 430 Russian Jews lived in Boston. In 1910, Russian immigrants totaled 64,283 (Stack, *International Conflict,* 23–4). On the effort to restrict immigration, see Barbara M. Solomon, *Ancestors and Immigrants: A Changing New England Tradition* (Cambridge: Harvard University Press, 1956).

5. For social and economic mobility information, see Stephan Thernstrom, *The Other Bostonians: Poverty and Progress in the American Metropolis, 1880–1970* (Cambridge: Harvard University Press, 1973). Thernstrom limits his analysis to men.

6. For an insightful reading of ethnic politics in Boston see James J. Connolly, *The Triumph of Ethnic Progressivism: Urban Political Culture in Boston, 1900–1925* (Cambridge: Harvard University Press, 1998). In her study on Boston women, Sarah Deutsch brings together important information on the political status of blacks, arguing that blacks lost political influence beginning in the 1890s, when, as a result of redistricting, they lost their seat in the Massachusetts House of Representatives and control over a City Council seat. Even with the realignment and mobilization of the Democratic Party in the late 1920s and 1930s, blacks did not gain significant political influence, despite their

efforts; see *Women and the City: Gender, Space, and Power in Boston, 1870–1940* (New York: Oxford University Press, 2000), 264–83. On Boston's blacks, see John Daniels, *In Freedom's Birthplace* (1914; reprinted, New York: Arno Press, 1969); Elizabeth H. Pleck, *Black Migration and Poverty: Boston, 1865–1900* (New York: Academic Press, 1979); Richard Alan Ballou, "Even in Freedom's Birthplace: The Development of Boston's Black Ghetto, 1900–1940," (Ph.D. diss., University of Michigan, 1984); and Adelaide M. Cromwell, *The Other Brahmins: Boston's Black Upper Class, 1750–1950* (Fayetteville: University of Arkansas Press, 1994).

7. Connolly outlines what he calls the "political reconstruction of Boston's ethnic character," arguing that as Irish Catholics gained greater political control in the city, social relations as well as politics were transformed, an observation that this book corroborates (Connolly, *Triumph of Ethnic Progressivism*, 4–5). Beginning in 1879, women had been allowed to elect members to and to serve on the school board, but they were otherwise disenfranchised until the federal amendment. In the final effort to secure the vote, women unified across class and ethnic lines; however, they engaged along partisan lines once the victory was won (Deutsch, *Women and the City*, 219–83). On political mobilization and realignment in the 1930s, see Gerald H. Gamm, *The Making of New Deal Democrats: Voting Behavior and Realignment in Boston, 1920–1940* (Chicago: University of Chicago Press, 1989), 45–73. For discussions of Boston politics in the context of Massachusetts history, see Richard D. Brown and Jack Tager, *Massachusetts: A Concise History* (Amherst: University of Massachusetts Press, 2000), 260–74, and J. Joseph Huthmacher, *Massachusetts People and Politics, 1919–1933* (Cambridge: Harvard University Press, 1959), 14–16.

8. I am indebted to Sarah Deutsch for uncovering hard-to-find information on services for the poor among Boston's black population (*Women and the City*, 42–4). The quotation is from Daniels, *In Freedom's Birthplace*, 213. Because of the small size of Boston's black population and the more informal organization of black charitable effort at the time, I have not provided a formal comparison between black and white charitable endeavors.

9. The average percentage of foreign-stock population in the ten largest cities was 53.4. Boston, with 71.5 percent, was not far from New York (73.3), Cleveland (64.9), and Chicago (64.4). Cities closer to the average were Detroit (57.6), Pittsburgh (51.1), and Philadelphia (50.6). Only three of these largest cities were below the average: Los Angeles (36.8), St. Louis (35.1), and Baltimore (29.1). In Boston, Irish immigrants and children of Irish immigrants far outnumbered other immigrant groups, and Italians, Russian Jews, and Slavic groups were comparatively smaller than in other, more industrial cities. Moreover, the size of Boston's nonwhite population was much smaller than the average nonwhite population of other big cities. In 1910, Boston's nonwhite residents constituted only 2.2 percent of the population, and they reached only 2.6 percent by 1930, when the average for big cities was 9.4; see Bruce Stave, *The New Deal and the Last Hurrah: Pittsburgh Machine Politics* (Pittsburgh: University of Pittsburgh Press, 1970), 41; Charles H. Trout,

Boston, the Great Depression, and the New Deal (New York: Oxford University Press, 1977), 11; Commonwealth of Massachusetts, *Census of Massachusetts, 1910.*

Chapter 1. Boston's Charity System

1. For a list of charities in Boston at the beginning of the twentieth century, see Commonwealth of Massachusetts, *Annual Report of the State Board of Charity* (Boston, 1901). Boston had numerous charitable institutions, both public and private. These included an almshouse, homes for the aged, orphanages, homes for unwed mothers, hospitals, and settlement houses. Focusing on "outdoor relief," this book does not examine the history of Boston's charitable institutions. Studies of some of these institutions include: Brian Gratton, *Urban Elders: Family, Work, and Welfare among Boston's Aged, 1890–1950* (Philadelphia: Temple University Press, 1986); Eric C. Schneider, *In the Web of Class: Delinquents and Reformers in Boston, 1810s–1930s* (New York: New York University Press, 1992); Peter C. Holloran, *Boston's Wayward Children: Social Services for Homeless Children, 1830–1930* (Boston: Northeastern University Press, 1994); and Matthew A. Crenson, *Building the Invisible Orphanage: A Prehistory of the American Welfare System* (Cambridge: Harvard University Press, 1998). Sarah Deutsch vividly describes the effort by poor women to piece together charity; see *Women and the City: Gender, Space, and Power in Boston, 1870–1940* (New York: Oxford University Press, 2000), 25–53.

2. Boston Council of Social Agencies, *Bulletin* 5, no. 2 (February 1926): 11; Overseers of the Poor (OP), *Annual Report, 1908.*

3. Deutsch documents the activism of women in Boston's many reform organizations in *Women and the City* and stresses their increased influence. Other studies on women's reform efforts include Lori D. Ginzberg, *Women and the Work of Benevolence: Morality, Politics and Class in Nineteenth-Century United States* (New Haven: Yale University Press, 1990), and Robyn L. Muncy, *Creating a Female Dominion in American Reform, 1890–1930* (New York: Oxford University Press, 1991). Focusing on women, these works underplay the role of men in social reform and benevolent organizations.

4. On the nonsectarian charity movement in Boston, see Nathan Irvin Huggins, *Protestants against Poverty: Boston's Charities, 1870–1900* (Westport, Conn.: Greenwood, 1971). It might be more correct to call these nonsectarian organizations "Protestant-led" since they did not have formal ties with any Protestant denomination and did not restrict their charity to Protestants; however, in leadership and in philosophy, they were Protestant organizations. This group included Congregationalists, Episcopalians, Presbyterians, and white Methodists. Black Protestants are not included in this grouping since they were segregated in their own institutions and were largely excluded from the nonsectarian charity movement.

5. Eighteen nationalities were represented among these foreign-born charity cases. Associated Charities (AC), *Annual Report,* 1917; on Pear, see "Service Today for W. H. Pear," *Boston Herald,* August 6, 1954.

6. On the scientific charity movement, see Walter I. Trattner, *From Poor Law to Welfare State: A History of Social Welfare in America*, 6th ed. (New York: Free Press, 1999), 77–103.

7. Boston Provident Association (BPA), *Annual Report*, 1911; AC, *Annual Report*, 1910.

8. AC, *Annual Report*, 1911.

9. AC, *Annual Report*, 1910. At its founding, the Associated Charities had criticized the Provident Association for providing relief to the poor. On this controversy, see Huggins, *Protestants against Poverty*, 57–81.

10. In 1879, Philadelphia abolished its public outdoor relief program and relied on private benevolent organizations to administer public moneys to the needy. In New York, Josephine Shaw Lowell became a leading spokeswoman for the elimination of public outdoor relief. On Philadelphia, see William H. Pear, *The Philadelphia Relief Study* (Philadelphia: Committee on the Philadelphia Relief Study, 1926); on New York, see Barry J. Kaplan, "Reformers and Charity: The Abolition of Public Relief in New York City, 1870–1898," *Social Service Review* 52 (1978): 202–14; on Lowell, see Trattner, *From Poor Law to Welfare State*, 95–6. On the relationship between the nonsectarian charities and the Overseers, see Pear, "How Boston Meets and Supports Its Family Service Program," *Proceedings of the National Conference of Social Work*, 1925, 482–98.

11. In her study of welfare in Chicago, Joanne Goodwin also found that many reformers supported the wage work of poor women. She does not identify this attitude as being more pronounced among Protestants, although many of her examples are men and women with ties to Protestant "nonsectarian" charities and institutions; see *Gender and the Politics of Welfare Reform: Mothers' Pensions in Chicago, 1911–1929* (Chicago: University of Chicago Press, 1997). In likening these charity efforts to the emergence of feminism, I rely on Nancy F. Cott's conception of feminism as a cultural and intellectual shift as much as a social and political movement; see *The Grounding of Modern Feminism* (New Haven: Yale University Press, 1987).

12. On the Catholic Charitable Bureau, see Dorothy M. Brown and Elizabeth McKeown, *The Poor Belong to Us: Catholic Charities and American Welfare* (Cambridge: Harvard University Press, 1997); Susan S. Walton, "To Preserve the Faith: Catholic Charities in Boston, 1870–1930," in *Catholic Boston: Studies in Religion and Community, 1870–1970*, ed. Robert E. Sullivan and James M. O'Toole (Boston: Roman Catholic Archbishop of Boston, 1985), 67–119; and Daniel McLellan, "History of the Catholic Charitable Bureau of the Archdiocese of Boston" (Ph.D. diss., University of Notre Dame, 1984). Sisters operated Catholic orphanages, schools, homes for unwed mothers, and asylums. On their work, see Mary J. Oates, "'The Good Sisters': The Work and Position of Catholic Churchwomen in Boston, 1870–1940," in *Catholic Boston*, 171–200. Focusing on outdoor relief, this book does not examine the impact of the Catholic Charitable Bureau on the institutional work of the sisters. Books that consider the ways that Catholic institutions fostered a "subculture" are James M. O'Toole, *Militant and Triumphant: William Henry O'Connell and the Catholic Church in Boston, 1859–1944* (Notre Dame, Ind.: University of

Notre Dame, 1992), and Paula M. Kane, *Separatism and Subculture: Boston Catholicism, 1900–1920* (Chapel Hill: University of North Carolina Press, 1994).

13. Walton, "To Preserve the Faith," 93. The placement of children into foster homes was a pressing issue because Massachusetts led the country in abolishing orphanages; see Crenson, *Building the Invisible Orphanage,* 254. Catholic organizations on the national level also responded guardedly to idea of mothers' pensions because many advocates of these pensions saw them as a way to curb the growth of Catholic orphanages. Eventually, the National Conference of Catholic Charities joined the broad movement for public support of dependent children in their own homes but only after it was assured it could influence the parameters of the proposals; see Brown and McKeown, *The Poor Belong to Us,* 120–5, and Crenson, *Building the Invisible Orphanage,* 246–83.

14. Walton, "To Preserve the Faith," 68; Kane, *Separatism and Subculture,* 61.

15. The CCB reported that "absence of the mother" was the most common reason children were removed from a home; see Commonwealth of Massachusetts, *Report of the Commission on the Support of Dependent Minor Children of Widowed Mothers* (Boston, January 1913), 69. Between 1900 and 1910, women made up 21 percent of the workforce nationally while in Boston they made up 31 percent. On this and Catholic attitudes toward men's and women's roles, see Kane, *Separatism and Subculture,* 244–8.

16. Kane, *Separatism and Subculture,* 247; Brown and McKeown, *The Poor Belong to Us,* 72–74; Daniel J. Walkowitz, "The Making of a Feminized Professional Identity: Social Work in the 1920s," *American Historical Review* 95 (October 1990): 1051–75.

17. For a history of the Federated, see Barbara M. Solomon, *Pioneers in Service: The History of the Associated Jewish Philanthropies of Boston* (Boston: Associated Jewish Philanthropies, 1956).

18. Solomon Friedman was the first Jewish member of the Overseers, and Marcus Kallman was the first Jewish visitor. According to Solomon, Kallman was "valued for his facility in Yiddish and German"; see Solomon, *The History of the Associated Jewish Philanthropies,* 13.

19. Federated Jewish Charities, *Annual Report,* 1912.

20. The Hebrew word for giving to the poor is *zedakah,* which means "righteousness" or "justice." The Federated embodied this philosophy and understood charity to be as much an obligation of the giver as a need of the poor. "Charity," *Encylclopadedia Judaica,* vol. 5 (New York: Macmillan, 1971), 338–54.

21. Information on the history and structure of the Overseers is included in the *Reports of the Boston Finance Commission,* 1922, 1932, and in the *Annual Reports* of the Overseers of the Poor. The Board ran a Temporary Home for Women and a municipal lodging house, called the Wayfarers' Lodge, for men. Both institutions provided temporary shelter, basic health care, and employment referral. The primary function of the Overseers, however, was the dispersal of public relief funds.

22. "Members of the Board from its Reorganization in 1864," Boston Welfare Department, *Annual Report,* 1964, 22–6. On the appointment of women to the Overseers, see

"Women as Overseers of Poor," *Woman's Journal*, May 22, 1897, 162. Sarah Deutsch discusses the success that many native-born women had in gaining appointments on city and state boards in the late nineteenth century though she interprets their influence as more significant than I do; see Deutsch, *Women and the City*, 220–33.

23. Settlement was a complex legal status, usually requiring five years of continuous residency and tax payment, in the form of either property tax or poll tax. Under Massachusetts law, a community could charge another city or town for the poor relief for any person found to have had "settlement" there. If settlement could not be determined, the state bore the cost of the support. Robert W. Kelso, *The History of Public Poor Relief in Massachusetts, 1620–1920* (Boston: Houghton Mifflin, 1922); the quotation on the economy of poor relief is from the Overseers' retirement testimonial for Benjamin Pettee, OP, *Annual Report*, 1914–15, 17.

24. OP, *Annual Report*, 1906. The twentieth-century records of Boston's Overseers of the Poor were destroyed, and so it is difficult to provide more than a profile of the department's recipients and activities. The information here comes from the department's *Annual Reports* and special reports by the Boston Finance Commission during the 1920s, specifically, Boston Finance Commission, *Reports and Communications*, vol. 18 (Boston, 1923–4). A 1925 report on old age pensions reported that women made up 82 percent of the public aid recipients 65 and over; see *Report on Old-Age Pensions* (Boston, 1925), 105. Brian Gratton's work on Boston's old age homes shows that institutional care was more common for elderly men than for elderly women. He argues that relief officers were more willing to give outdoor relief to women than to men; see *Urban Elders*, 136.

25. OP, *Annual Report*, 1905–6.

26. This percentage is based on amounts distributed by the Overseers of the Poor, as reported in their annual reports, and on figures on municipal finances found in Commonwealth of Massachusetts, *Annual Reports of the Statistics of Municipal Finance*, published in Boston beginning in 1906.

Chapter 2. Mothers' Aid, 1910–1919

1. Roy Lubove, *The Struggle for Social Security, 1900–1935* (Cambridge: Harvard University Press, 1968), 91–112; Mark Leff, "Consensus for Reform: The Mothers'-Pension Movement in the Progressive Era," *Social Service Review* 47 (September 1973): 397–417; Walter I. Trattner, *From Poor Law to Welfare State*, 6th ed. (New York: Free Press, 1999), 222–6. There are significant interpretive differences among historians of women who have written about widows' pensions. Some scholars writing in the 1970s and 1980s viewed this early welfare program for women as merely an extension of patriarchal control over women's lives. Examples of this interpretation are: Mimi Abramovitz, *Regulating the Lives of Women: Social Welfare Policy from Colonial Times to the Present* (Boston: South End Press, 1988); Janet Marie Wedel, "The Origins of State Patriarchy during the Progressive Era: A Sociological Study of the Mothers' Aid Movement" (Ph.D. diss., Wash-

ington University, St. Louis, 1975); and Libba Gage Moore, "Mothers' Pensions: The Origins of the Relationship between Women and the Welfare State" (Ph.D. diss., University of Massachusetts, 1986). Later studies presented this welfare program as a product of women's activism that offered needed assistance to poor women even as it reflected and, in some ways, reinforced gender inequality. Examples of this interpretation are Molly Ladd-Taylor, *Mother-Work: Women, Child Welfare, and the State, 1890–1930* (Chicago: University of Illinois Press, 1994), 135–66, and Linda Gordon, *Pitied but Not Entitled: Single Mothers and the History of Welfare* (New York: Free Press, 1994), 37–64. The literature by sociologists includes Ann Shola Orloff, "The Political Origins of America's Belated Welfare State," in *The Politics of Social Policy in the United States,* ed. Margaret Weir, Ann Shola Orloff, and Theda Skocpol (Princeton: Princeton University Press, 1988), 37–80, and Theda Skocpol, *Protecting Soldiers and Mothers: The Political Origins of Social Policy in the United States* (Cambridge: Harvard University Press, 1992). The notable exceptions are Joanne L. Goodwin, *Gender and the Politics of Welfare Reform: Mothers' Pensions in Chicago, 1911–1929* (Chicago: University of Chicago Press, 1997), and Matthew A. Crenson, *Building the Invisible Orphanage: A Prehistory of the American Welfare State* (Cambridge: Harvard University Press, 1998). Studying Chicago, Goodwin found that mothers' pensions marked a significant growth of public aid that operated beyond the control of partisan politics. She attributed this to the power of women's interests groups in Chicago, particularly the network of women associated with Hull House, which ensured that the program was implemented outside the control of local politicians. Surprisingly, Goodwin offers little reflection on the meaning of nonpartisanship in the context of ethnic politics and competing religious groups; nevertheless, she provides important information on the development and implementation of Mothers' Aid in one locality with special attention to the ways the program evolved into a wage subsidy rather than a pension. Looking at several locations, particularly New York, Crenson explores mothers' pensions in connection with the trend away from institutional care of poor children and examines the ways competing religious groups reacted to the movement away from orphanages. He argues that the religious conflicts surrounding "home care" were eventually resolved by limiting the scope of most widows' aid programs. Goodwin's and Crenson's studies demonstrate the importance of local political and religious conflicts to the formation and implementation of Mothers' Aid, an observation that the history of Mothers' Aid in Boston corroborates.

2. Some of the varying interpretations of maternalism are gathered in the anthology edited by Seth Koven and Sonya Michel, *Mothers of a New World: Maternalist Politics and the Origins of Welfare States* (New York: Routledge, 1993). Kathryn Kish Sklar's "Historical Foundations of Women's Power" in that volume is an example of an interpretation of maternalism as a class-bridging concept. Linda Gordon's work forwards a more critical interpretation of maternalism; see *Pitied but Not Entitled,* 55–6. Comparative studies of "maternal" and "paternal" welfare regimes include Seth Koven and Sonya Michel, "'Womanly Duties': Maternalist Politics and the Origins of Welfare States in France,

Germany, Great Britain, and the United States, 1880–1920," *American Historical Review* 95 (1990): 1076–108; and Skocpol, *Protecting Soldiers and Mothers.*

3. Massachusetts was only one of twenty states that instituted public aid programs for needy mothers and children between 1911 and 1913; by 1920, forty states had Mothers' Aid programs. Most states restricted aid to widows, but some funded deserted and divorced mothers. A few states aided unmarried mothers and mothers whose husbands were too incapacitated or ill to support the family. The administration of Mothers' Aid programs also varied, with some localities operating the program through juvenile courts, others establishing independent boards, and some, including Massachusetts, relying on the offices of the public poor relief program to implement the state's Mothers' Aid program. Mothers' Aid became the model for the Aid to Dependent Children program enacted by the Social Security Act of 1935. For overviews of the national effort to create mothers' pensions, see Ladd-Taylor, *Mother-Work;* Skocpol, *Protecting Soldiers and Mothers;* Gordon, *Pitied but Not Entitled;* and Goodwin, *Gender and the Politics.* Although they group and label the women's organizations differently, they conclude that the movement for mothers' pensions represented an attempt to bridge class differences between women which gained the support of a wide range of women's organizations, some conservative and others feminist. Male labor leaders and social insurance advocates endorsed the idea of mothers' pensions, but they did not campaign for their passage. On the difference between the campaigns for social insurance and widows' pensions, see Linda Gordon, "Social Insurance and Public Assistance: The Influence of Gender in Welfare Thought in the United States," *American Historical Review* 97 (February 1992): 19–54, and Skocpol, *Protecting Soldiers and Mothers,* 428–32.

4. Articles supporting widows' pensions also appeared in *Good Housekeeping* and *Collier's;* see Skocpol, *Protecting Soldiers and Mothers,* 432–9, and Leff, "Consensus for Reform," 406. On competing rationales for mothers' pensions, see Edna Bullock, ed., *Selected Articles on Mothers' Pensions* (New York: H. W. Wilson, 1915). On mothers' pensions and wage work, see Goodwin, *Gender and the Politics,* 48–51.

5. Gordon, *Pitied but Not Entitled,* 37–64. In her work on Chicago, Goodwin highlights the effort by some advocates, a group she calls "social justice feminists," to couple support for Mothers' Aid with efforts to improve women's wages and working conditions in ways decidedly less conservative. She admits that this coalition was somewhat exceptional; see *Gender and the Politics,* 45–7.

6. Skocpol cites the "fear of corruption" as an impediment to the formation of social provision programs in this country. She does not, however, link that fear to the success of women's reform efforts, but, instead, argues that the grassroots organizational structure of women's political activism explains the legislative success of programs for women; see *Protecting Soldiers and Mothers,* 311–20.

7. In her work on welfare, Linda Gordon stresses the ability of aid recipients often to subvert welfare programs in ways unintended by those formulating policy. See *Heroes of*

Their Own Lives: The History of Politics of Family Violence (New York: Viking, 1988) and "What Does Welfare Regulate?" *Social Research* 55, no. 4 (1988): 609–47.

8. On the Congress of Mothers, see Ladd-Taylor, *Mother-Work*, 139–43; Skocpol, *Protecting Soldiers and Mothers*, 445–56; Goodwin, *Gender and the Politics*, 27–31; National Congress of Mothers, *Child-Welfare Magazine* 8 (1913): 143 and *Child-Welfare Magazine* 5 (1911): 140. On the conservatism of Massachusetts politics at this time, see Richard Abrams, *Conservatism in a Progressive Era: Massachusetts Politics, 1900–1912* (Cambridge: Harvard University Press, 1964).

9. Clara Cahill Park, "Wanted—Rooseveltian Landlords," *Child-Welfare Magazine* 5 (1911): 58–9; "Widows' Pension in Massachusetts," *Child-Welfare Magazine* 10 (June 1912): 343–6.

10. Clara C. Park, "Helping the Widowed Mother to Keep a Home," *Home Progress* (April 1913): 43–8.

11. The rabbi's speech was reported in the "State News" section of *Child-Welfare Magazine* 6, no. 6 (February 1912): 209; Boston *Globe*, January 2, 1912; and *Boston Herald*, January 2, 1912.

12. Letter to the editor, *Survey* 30 (August 1913): 669.

13. Park, "Helping the Widowed Mother to Keep a Home, " 44; emphasis is Park's.

14. The Massachusetts campaign was reported in *Child-Welfare Magazine* 6 (February 1912): 209–10; 8 (April 1913): 305; 9 (May 1912): 316; 10 (June 1912): 358; 12 (August 1912): 436.

15. The reaction of leaders of Boston's Catholic and Jewish charities was similar to the reaction by Catholic and Jewish leaders in other cities; see Crenson, *Building the Invisible Orphanage*, 266–7, 271–80. Skocpol also found evidence that Jewish charity leaders in New York were early supporters of mothers' pensions; see *Protecting Mothers and Soldiers*, 667.

16. Grace Abbott was among the first to advance the history of welfare as struggle between public and private, and historians of social welfare have duplicated this argument; see *From Relief to Social Security* (Chicago: University of Chicago Press, 1941); Lubove, *Struggle*, 103–6; Trattner, *From Poor Law*, 223–5; and Leff, "Consensus for Reform." On the national level, the Conference of Charities and Corrections and the Russell Sage Foundation opposed widows' pensions; see Skocpol, *Protecting Soldiers and Mothers*, 425. For an example of their opposition, see C. C. Carsten, "Public Pensions to Widows with Children," *Survey* 29 (January 4, 1913): 459–66. Carsten was the secretary of the Massachusetts Society for the Prevention of Cruelty to Children.

17. Clara Cahill Park, "Widows' Pension in Massachusetts," *Child-Welfare Magazine* 11 (June 1912): 343–6.

18. *Boston Evening Transcript*, February 28, 1913.

19. Commonwealth of Massachusetts, *Report of the Commission on the Support of Dependent Minor Children of Widowed Mothers*, House Document 2075 (Boston, 1913).

20. A number of Protestant agencies criticized the tabulation of the commission's survey and sent letters of complaint to the commission. One, for example, from the director of the Society for the Care of Girls, read, "I think there must be some mistake in regard to your opinion of the cards [information] that we sent to your office. When the children have been removed it has always been because of the absolute unfitness of the parents to keep the children"; letter, October 21, 1912, in *Report of the Commission,* 85.

21. Commonwealth of Massachusetts, *Report of the Commission,* 20.

22. Commonwealth of Massachusetts, *Report of the Commission,* 31.

23. Commonwealth of Massachusetts, *Report of the Commission,* 35.

24. Commonwealth of Massachusetts, *Report of the Commission,* 35.

25. Letter from Parker B. Field of the Children's Mission to the commission, October 29, 1912, in *Report of the Commission,* 80.

26. Letters in *Report of the Commission,* 81, 84–5, 79.

27. Porter R. Lee, "The Massachusetts Report on the Relief of Widows," *Survey* 30 (1913): 134–6, quotations from 136, 135; William Pear in Lee, "The Massachusetts Report," 135.

28. Robert F. Forester, "Communications," *Survey* 30 (1913): 253–4. Several women's organizations in Boston, including the Daughters of the American Revolution and the Ladies Aid and Missionary Society, petitioned the state legislature to pass the Widows' Subsidies Bill. These petitions are in the legislative packet for the Mothers' Aid Bill at the Massachusetts Archives.

29. Robert W. Kelso, "Promoter of Social Legislation," *The Family* (December 1920): 11–12.

30. The drafters included: Zilpha Smith, director of the Boston School of Social Work; Alice Higgins, general secretary of the Associated Charities; J. Prentice Murphy, general secretary of the Children's Aid Society; Parker B. Field, general secretary of the Children's Mission; C. C. Carsten, general secretary of the Massachusetts Society for the Prevention of Cruelty to Children; and William H. Pear, general agent of the Boston Provident Association. William H. Pear, "My Recollection of the Writing of the Massachusetts Mothers' Aid Law," November 1938, William H. Pear Papers, Simmons College Archives; letter to the editor from William H. Pear, *Boston Evening Transcript,* February 26, 1913. The legislative committee made no substantial changes to the social workers proposal, although the committee delayed implementation until the following September. The mark-up of the bill is part of the legislative packet for the Mothers' Aid bill at the Massachusetts Archives. The new bill was inroduced as H2404. It committed the commonwealth to funding a third of the assistance distributed by the program.

31. In 1924, the Congress of Mothers became the Parent Teacher Association (PTA), and Clara Cahill Park left the Massachusetts Congress of Mothers in 1914 when she left the Boston area. Linda Gordon and Molly Ladd-Taylor are critical of the maternal politics of the Progressive era while Theda Skocpol is more celebratory of the effort by middle-class women to influence welfare programs for women. All three, nevertheless,

see a waning of political action by and for women toward the end of the Progressive era and in the 1920s; see Gordon, *Pitied but Not Entitled*, 60–4; Ladd-Taylor, *Mother-Work*, 159–60; and Skocpol, *Protecting Soldeirs and Mothers*, 543–39. Paula Baker identifies the same retreat from political activism by women's organizations, but she relates it to women's suffrage; see "The Domestication of Politics," *American Historical Review* 89 (June 1984): 620–47. Studying Chicago, Joanne Goodwin argues that the network of "social justice feminists," including those at Hull House and in the newly established federal Children's Bureau, persisted in their support for mothers' pensions well into the 1920s; see *Gender and the Politics*, 151.

32. Commonwealth of Massachusetts, State Board of Charity, *Annual Report* (Boston, 1914).

33. William Goodhue, State Board of Charity, *Annual Report* (Boston, 1913), 133. For the policies of the Mothers' Aid program, see State Board of Charity, *Annual Report* (Boston, 1914), 128–34, and Ada Eliot Sheffield, "Administration of Mothers' Aid in Massachusetts," *Survey* 31 (1913–14): 644–5, 659; a 1918 study showed that most of the families in the program had been poor before the death, illness, or departure of the father. While the fathers represented all occupational areas, skilled and unskilled "laborers" made up the largest single occupational category. In half the cases, the husbands had been earning only between $10 and $20 a week, at a time when the subsistence level for a family of four was $15 a week. Commonwealth of Massachusetts, *Report of the Special Commission on Social Insurance* (Boston, 1918).

34. Ada Sheffield, "Administration," 645; Commonwealth of Massachusetts, *Report of the Special Commission on Social Insurance* (Boston, 1918); "Boston," in U.S. Department of Labor, Children's Bureau, *Standards of Public Aid to Children in Their Own Homes*, by Florence Nesbitt, no. 118 (Washington, D.C., 1923), 91–103; Overseers of the Poor, *Annual Report*, 1914–1920; Sheffield, "Administration," 644; on boarders, see Alice L. Higgins, secretary, and Florence Windom, agent, Associated Charities of Boston, "Helping Widows to Bring Up Children," *Proceedings of the National Conference on Charities and Corrections* (1910): 138–44. In her work on family violence, Linda Gordon has shown that some male boarders posed a threat to the safety of women and girls; however, she concluded that the effort by charity officials to regulate the household formation of poor families was primarily a means of controlling the private lives of poor women; see Linda Gordon, *Heroes of Their Own Lives: The Politics and History of Family Violence: Boston: 1880–1960* (New York: Viking, 1988).

35. Commonwealth of Massachusetts, State Board of Charity, *Annual Report* (Boston, 1913), 129–30. Joanne Goodwin's work on Chicago shows that mothers' pensions in Illinois were also designed to operate as a wage subsidy and that poor women, particularly African American women, were expected to combine support from wage work with the pension. See Goodwin, "An Experiment in Paid Motherhood: The Implementation of Mothers' Pensions in Early Twentieth Century Chicago," *Gender and History* 4 (autumn 1992): 323–42. Detailed case records for the Mothers' Aid program in Boston do not

exist, making an assessment of cases along ethnic and racial lines impossible. A log of names from the program's first year of operation suggests that women with Irish surnames received larger grants than Italian women, but the reasons for the differential are impossible to ascertain from the records; see Massachusetts Archives, Department of Public Welfare Collection.

36. U.S. Department of Labor, Children's Bureau, *Standards of Public Aid,* 96–7; Ada Eliot Sheffield, "The Influence of Mothers' Aid upon Family Life," *Survey* 34 (1915): 378–9. On Gordon's analysis of "maternalism," see her "Gender, State and Society: A Debate with Theda Skocpol," *Contention* 2 (spring 1993): 139–56.

37. The family was counted as foreign-born if the father was listed as such. In the majority of cases statewide (56.9 percent), the father had been foreign-born. Families of Irish-born fathers made up 18.3 percent of the total population of cases; Canadians, 12.9; Russian Jews, 6.5; Italians, 4.9; English, 4; and other nationalities, 10.3. In Boston, the percentage of cases considered foreign-born was even higher, calculated in 1923 as 66 percent of the city's Mothers' Aid cases. Here, the three largest immigrant groups using Mothers' Aid were Irish, Russian, and Italian, each representing a third of the foreign-born Mothers' Aid cases in the city. Both statewide and in Boston, the number of immigrants using Mothers' Aid was disproportionate to their numbers in the population, and in Boston, the percentage of Russian and Italian families receiving Mothers' Aid was disproportionate to their percentage of the immigrant population. Commonwealth of Massachusetts, State Board of Charity, *Annual Report,* 1913; Commonwealth of Massachusetts, *Report of the Special Commission on Social Insurance* (Boston, 1918); "Boston," in U.S. Department of Labor, Children's Bureau, *Standards of Public Aid,* 91–103. No racial breakdown of cases was made in these studies of Mothers' Aid in Boston.

38. In 1914, expenditures on Mothers' Aid were $248,602; in 1919, they were $586,341, a 136 percent increase. Expenditures per case were $244 in 1914 and $366 in 1919. Adjusted for the cost of living, the increase was more modest (24 percent), but it nevertheless kept ahead of the inflation associated with wartime. Overseers of the Poor, *Annual Report* (Boston), 1914–19; expenditures on Dependent Aid were $178,603 in 1914; they were $240,521 in 1919. Adjusted for the cost of living, this represented a 29 percent decrease.

39. Edward T. Hartman, "Plucking the Massachusetts State Board of Charity," *Survey* 33 (1914–15): 552; new visitors included Mary A. Mulloney, Margaret A. Murphy, and Susan T. O'Connor (Commonwealth of Massachusetts, Board of Charity, *Annual Report,* 1915).

40. U.S. Department of Labor, Children's Bureau, *Proceedings of the Conference on Mothers' Pensions, June 28, 1922, Providence, Rhode Island,* no. 109 (Washington, D.C., 1922), 21.

41. Commonwealth of Massachusetts, State Board of Public Welfare, *Annual Report,* 1923, 9.

42. Commonwealth of Massachusetts, State Board of Public Welfare, *Annual Report,* 1924, 8–9.

43. Commonwealth of Massachusetts, State Board of Charity, *Annual Report,* 1918, 120.

44. U.S. Department of Labor, Children's Bureau, "Standard of Public Aid," 93. The Overseers, nevertheless, submitted cases to the new department in order to receive partial reimbursement, and they complained when cases were rejected; see Overseers of the Poor, *Annual Report,* 1915.

45. Overseers of the Poor, *Annual Report,* 1914.

46. Boston Provident Association, *Annual Report,* 1914–15; Associated Charities, *Annual Report,* 1914.

47. Boston Provident Association, *Annual Report,* 1914–15; Associated Charities, *Annual Report,* 1914.

48. On Silverman, see Barbara Solomon, *Pioneers in Service: The History of the Associated Jewish Philanthropies of Boston* (Boston: Associated Jewish Philanthropies, 1956), 77; Ferdinand Berl, "History of the Jewish Community of Boston," 54; Papers of the Combined Jewish Philanthropies (PCJP), box 1, folder 4, American Jewish Historical Society; Federated Jewish Charities, *Report of the Welfare Committee,* 1919, 5, PCJP, box 3, folder 2.

49. Catholic Charitable Bureau, Annual Report, 1922, Catholic Charitable Bureau Files, Archives of the Archdiocese of Boston.

Chapter 3. Politics and Public Welfare, 1920–1929

1. By law, all poor mothers with dependent children under the age of 14 (raised to 16 in 1924) could receive Mothers' Aid. In practice, the program excluded all single mothers and mothers deemed "unfit." See chapter 2.

2. This book compares specific aid programs to correct the notion that the expansion of public welfare programs was a knit-together expression of modern liberalism. Barbara Nelson and Linda Gordon have also provided valuable comparisons between the public assistance programs and social insurance programs that developed in the early twentieth century, and Theda Skocpol has made even broader comparisons between programs meant to serve men and those supporting women. These scholars and others have alerted us to the significant differences in assumption, implementation, and outcome of the various programs that provided social provisions to Americans. However, none of these comparisons considers the influence of urban politics—specifically ethnic and religious conflict—on the formulation and implementation of welfare programs at the local level. Joanne Goodwin's study of mothers' pensions in Chicago, and her comparisons of that program with Dependent Aid, is an important exception; however, her conclusion that the mothers' pension program there was removed from local politics through the effort of female reformers, particularly those associated with Hull House, obscures how the attempt to remove a program from the "taint" of local political conflict was itself political. Barbara J. Nelson, "The Origin of the Two-Channel Welfare State: Workmen's Compensation and Mothers' Aid," in *Women, the State, and Welfare,* ed. Linda Gordon (Madison:

University of Wisconsin Press, 1990), 123–51; Linda Gordon, "Social Insurance and Public Assistance: The Influence of Gender in Welfare Thought in the United States, 1890–1935," *American Historical Review* 97 (February 1992): 19–54; Theda Skocpol, *Protecting Soldiers and Mothers: The Political Origins of Social Policy in the United States* (Cambridge: Harvard University Press, 1992); Joanne Goodwin, *Gender and the Politics of Welfare Reform: Mothers' Pensions in Chicago, 1911–1929* (Chicago: University of Chicago Press, 1997).

3. On the enlarged definition of politics in the late nineteenth and early twentieth century, see Paula Baker, "The Domestication of Politics: Women and American Political Society, 1780–1920," *American Historical Review* 89 (June 1984): 620–47. Adjusted for the cost of living, the Overseers' payments to the poor rose 278 percent between 1912 and 1919. In 1912, the year before the passage of Mothers' Aid, the Overseers of the Poor distributed $108,197 directly to the poor; in 1919, they distributed $800,082 (a 639 percent increase). The information here, and throughout this chapter, on the expenditures by the Overseers of the Poor is from their annual reports. The Overseers of the Poor changed their name to the Overseers of the Public Welfare in 1922. Their annual reports were published separately and as part of the *Documents of the City of Boston, 1916–1941*. Calculations for cost-of-living adjustment use indexes gauged to the urban poor in Jeffrey G. Williamson and Peter H. Lindert, *American Inequality: A Macroeconomic History* (New York: Academic Press, 1980), 106, 111.

4. In 1910, 74 percent of Boston's population was either foreign-born or native-born of foreign parentage; see Commonwealth of Massachusetts, *Census of Massachusetts: 1910* (Boston, 1911), 890. On the emergence of antagonistic politics, see James J. Connolly, *The Triumph of Ethnic Progressivism: Urban Culture in Boston, 1900–1925* (Cambridge: Harvard University Press, 1998), 15–38; on Irish overrepresentation in politics, see John F. Stack Jr., *International Conflict in an American City: Boston's Irish, Italians, and Jews, 1935–1944* (Westport, Conn.: Greenwood Press, 1979), 33; on absence of an Irish political machine, see Charles H. Trout, "Curley of Boston: The Search for Irish Legitimacy," in *Boston 1700–1980: The Evolution of Urban Politics*, ed. Ronald P. Formisano and Constance K. Burns (Westport, Conn.: Greenwood Press, 1984), 165–95. Connolly argues that Progressive-era Boston history, as well as other urban histories, have been badly distorted by the notion of the ethnic machine versus reform, and he persuasively shows the speciousness of this dichotomy; see *The Triumph of Ethnic Progressivism*, 2, 7–8.

5. Connolly's research indicates that charter reform was not foisted upon the city by native-born reformers, but, in fact, enjoyed the support of many ethnic voters; nevertheless, the initiators of charter reform aimed to limit the influence of ward-level politicians, an increasing number of whom were Irish; see *The Triumph of Ethnic Progressivism*, 77–104. Also on charter reform, see Constance K. Burns, "The Irony of Progressive Reform: Boston, 1898–1910," in *Boston 1700–1980*, 133–64; Edward C. Banfield and Martha Derthick, *A Report on the Politics of Boston* (Cambridge: Joint Center for Urban Studies of the

Massachusetts Institute of Technology and Harvard University, 1960), 2. The Finance Commission predated the charter reform but was established as a permanent committee with the passage of the 1909 reforms.

6. Connolly provides an overview of the shifting interpretations of early twentieth century urban politics, tracing the literature from its initial criticism of ethnic leaders to its celebration of their urban liberalism; see *The Triumph of Ethnic Progressivism*, 193–7. Recent scholarship, including Connolly, suggests that the welfare function of ward politicians was limited. On this, see David P. Thelen, "Urban Politics: Beyond Bosses and Reformers," *Reviews in American History* 7 (1979): 406–12; Jon Teaford, "Finis for Tweed and Steffens: Rewriting the History of Urban Rule," *Reviews in American History* 10 (1982): 201–4; Craig Brown and Charles N. Halaby, "Machine Politics in America, 1870–1945," *Journal of Interdisciplinary History* 17 (1987): 587–612; and Terrence J. McDonald, *The Parameters of Urban Fiscal Policy: Socioeconomic Change and Political Culture in San Francisco, 1860–1906* (Berkeley: University of California Press, 1986). Thomas H. O'Connor includes the quotation by Lomasney in his popular history of Boston, *Bibles, Brahmins, and Bosses: A Short History of Boston* (Boston: Boston Public Library, 1991), 172. Some have questioned whether Lomasney ever made such a statement or, if he did, whether he meant it; nevertheless, it captures the shift in ideology that can rightly be attributed to the political context of early twentieth century Boston.

7. On Curley, see Jack Beatty, *The Rascal King: The Life and Times of James Michael Curley (1874–1958)* (Lexington, Mass.: Addison-Wesley, 1992); Charles H. Trout, "Curley of Boston: The Search for Irish Legitimacy," in *Boston, 1700–1980*, 165–95; Francis Russell, "The Last of the Bosses," *American Heritage* 10 (June 1959); and Joseph Dinneen, *The Purple Shamrock* (New York: W. W. Norton, 1949). Curley's life was also the basis for Edwin O'Connor's novel *The Last Hurrah* (Boston: Little, Brown, 1956), which was later made into a movie by the same title. On the limits of corruption, see Steven P. Erie, *Rainbow's End: Irish-Americans and the Dilemmas of Urban Machine Politics, 1840–1985* (Berkeley: University of California Press, 1988).

8. "Speech," *Proceedings of the City Council of the City of Boston (PCCB)*, February 5, 1917. Curley's support of the Mothers' Aid program is an example of what Connolly calls "ethnic progressivism." On this idea and Curley's expression of it, see *The Triumph of Ethnic Progressivism*, 133–60.

9. Economic status varied among groups of immigrants, but the differences did not follow a new/old immigrant model. The Irish were grouped occupationally similarly to the more newly arrived Italians. By contrast, the Eastern European immigrants, mostly Jews, arriving at the same time as the Italians, had an occupational pattern similar to British immigrants of the nineteenth century, with only 40 percent working as laborers and one-fourth in white-collar jobs. Only Boston's small black population saw less social and economic mobility than the Irish; see Thernstrom, *The Other Bostonians*, 176–219.

10. *PCCB*, April 17, 1922.

11. A gerrymander in 1915 put the Italian neighborhoods of the north, south, and west ends in territory controlled by Irish ward boss Martin Lomasney. No Italians served on the City Council or in the state legislature until after 1930. On this, see Charles H. Trout, *Boston, The Great Depression, and the New Deal* (New York: Oxford University Press, 1977), 41.

12. Quotations from *PCCB*, January 5, 1925. With the exception of the state-controlled school budget, all city appropriations originated from the mayor. The City Council could "reduce or reject any item . . . but without the approval of the Mayor [could] not increase any item in, nor the total of, a budget, nor add any item thereto, nor [could] it originate a budget"; "Amended City Charter of 1909," *Boston City Documents, 1929*, no. 36, 21–43.

13. *PCCB*, December 31, 1926; *Evening Transcript*, December 10, 1926; *Boston Post*, December 8, 1926; *Boston Evening Globe*, December 8, 1926; Curley is quoted in "Huge Cut in City Relief Denounced," *Boston Post*, December 8, 1926.

14. *PCCB*, April 17, 1922; *PCCB*, December 19, 1927; *PCCB*, November 9, 1925. A campaign was also under way at the state level to provide public aid to the elderly through old age pensions. In his study on Boston's elderly, *Urban Elders: Family, Work, and Welfare among Boston's Aged, 1890–1950* (Philadelphia: Temple University Press, 1986), Brian Gratton sees concern about the elderly as contributing to the increased expenditures on public welfare during the 1920s; however, in my examination of the *Proceedings of the City Council*, I found that unemployment more than the needs of the aged drove the expansion of public aid during the decade. On the movement for an Old Age Pension in Massachusetts, see Alton A. Linford, *Old Age Assistance in Massachusetts* (Chicago: University of Chicago Press, 1949), and Skocpol, *Protecting Soldiers and Mothers*, 267–72.

15. *PCCB*, December 19, 1927.

16. *PCCB*, December 19, 1927; *PCCB*, January 21, 1929; "Speech," *PCCB*, February 5, 1923.

17. Requesting ward-specific information became more common after 1924, when the City Council was reorganized; under the new system a representative was elected from each of the city wards. The Charter of 1909 had organized the City Council with nine members elected at large. For discussion about the published list, see *PCCB*, November 25, 1929.

18. Curley's appointments included John R. McVey, Margaret Leahy, Vincent de Paul Reade, Charles F. Hale, Thomas A. Forsyth, and Joseph A. Cummings during his first administration, and Frank Leveroni, Joseph F. Feeney, James J. Crowley, Grace M. Hurley, and Morris Bronstein during his second administration. The Board of Overseers hired Walter V. McCarthy in 1924.

19. *PCCB*, December 19, 1927.

20. *PCCB*, April 17, 1922.

21. *PCCB*, April 17, 1922; *PCCB*, December 19, 1927; *PCCB*, December 14, 1927. Until the 1890s, no woman served as an Overseer of the Poor; however, in the closing decade of

the nineteenth century, five women had been appointed to the Board of Overseers by Yankee administrations. Curley appointed no women to the board during his first term and only two during his second administration. Mayor Andrew Peters appointed three women during his administration (1918–22), and Mayor Malcolm Nichols (1926–30) appointed three as well; see "Members of the Board from Its Reorganization in 1864," Boston Welfare Department, *Annual Report*, 1964. In her work on women in Boston, Sarah Deutsch argues that the increased number of women political appointees in the 1890 transformed Boston's political space; however, she does not discuss the curtailing of their influence as the Irish took control. See *Women and the City: Gender, Space, and Power in Boston, 1870–1940* (New York: Oxford University Press, 2000), 220.

22. The Overseers had requested $75,000, and Peters sent a request for $70,000 to the City Council for approval; see *PCCB*, October 28, 1918. Caseloads for both Dependent Aid and Mothers' Aid decreased during Peters's administration, but only the Dependent Aid program saw a drop in expenditures; Mothers' Aid increased. Expenditures on Dependent Aid dropped from $259,256 in 1918 to $240,251 in 1919; expenditures on Mothers' Aid increased from $480,601 to $586,341 in 1919; see Overseers of the Poor, *Annual Report*, 1918, 1919. Expenditures on Dependent Aid were $264,971 in 1920 and $409,433 in 1921; expenditures on Mothers' Aid were $637,016 in 1920 and $715,091 in 1921; see Overseers of the Poor, *Annual Report*, 1920, 1921. While Peters was unable to control relief expenditures, the net charge to the city for these expenditures decreased during the four years of his administration. The net charge to the city had shown a steady increase between 1910 and 1917, and it resumed its upward trend after Peters left office. It did not show a decrease again until 1936. This suggests that Peters's policy of municipal efficiency pushed the Overseers to seek reimbursement for unsettled cases and for Mothers' Aid cases more aggressively from other cities and towns and from the commonwealth; see Overseers of the Poor, *Annual Report*, 1918–21. For details on the election in 1921, see Beatty, *Rascal King*, 219–28.

23. The state legislature passed a law in 1924 that prevented Boston's mayor from succeeding himself; on Nichols's election, see Beatty, *Rascal King*, 247. The Good Government Association was founded in 1903. Its founders included future Supreme Court Justice Louis D. Brandeis, merchant Edward A. Filene, and settlement house director Robert A. Woods. Its membership, however, was composed primarily of businessmen and lawyers. Campaigning against corruption and inefficiency in government, the association represented conservative business interests and called for limited government spending and a lower tax rate; see Connolly, *The Triumph of Ethnic Progressivism*, 41–7; Trout, *Boston*, 36, 43; "Speech," *PCCB*, January 4, 1926. The *Boston Daily Globe* reported Nichols's attitudes about public welfare as described by "Nichols's intimates"; see *Boston Daily Globe*, December 9, 1926, 1.

24. He appropriated $70,000 less than the department's expenditures the previous year ($2,446,076); see *PCCB*, April 11, 1927; *PCCB*, November 14, 1927; *PCCB*, December 13, 1926. Simon E. Hecht was originally appointed to the board in May 1908 by

Mayor George A. Hibbard; Frank Leveroni was appointed in May 1922 by Mayor Curley; James J. Crowley was appointed in October 1925 by Mayor Curley; and James H. Stone was appointed in December 1919 by Mayor Andrew J. Peters. Nichols replaced Hecht with Nathan Heller, another Jewish representative.

25. Boston Finance Commission, "Communication to the Mayor in Relation to the Overseers of the Public Welfare," *Reports,* 1923–24.

26. For a fuller history of the Finance Commission, see Burns, "The Irony of Progressive Reform," 148–53. The Finance Commission produced reports on the Overseers every year between 1915 and 1918, then again in 1922, 1923, and 1926.

27. Boston Finance Commission, "Communication to the Mayor in Relation to the Overseeing of the Public Welfare Department," *Reports,* 1922–23, 176–84.

28. The FinCom hired a professional woman social worker, former secretary of the Society for Organizing Charities in Providence, Rhode Island, to conduct the investigation for its more extensive report on the department; see Boston Finance Commission, *Reports,* 1922–23, 183.

29. In 1920, the expenditures on direct aid to the poor were $879,072; in 1929, they were $2,480,382, a 182 percent increase; if adjusted for the cost of living, it was a 219 percent increase. Total "payments," or operating expenses, of the city increased 56 percent during the same period; see Commonwealth of Massachusetts, *Annual Report on the Statistics of Municipal Finances,* 1920, 1929. While the caseload increased 107 percent, Boston's population increased only 8 percent that decade, from 747,000 in 1920 to 805,000 in 1929. The average annual expense per case was $244 in 1920 and $332 in 1929.

30. The Overseer's *Annual Reports* indicate that the unemployed became a significant proportion of poor relief cases during the 1920s. The high unemployment of the early 1920s appears to have sparked this trend. In 1921, 41 percent of Dependent Aid was related to unemployment. For the rest of the decade, unemployment cases remained approximately one-fourth of the Dependent Aid caseload. In contrast, in 1917 only 4 percent of cases, not covered by Mothers' Aid, had been a consequence of unemployment. OP, *Annual Reports,* 1917, 1920–29. In their reports, the Overseers did not distinguish between unemployed men and women. It can be assumed, though, that nearly all of the unemployed in the Dependent Aid program were men with families to support. In the early 1920s, the Finance Commission reported on the increase in spending on Dependent Aid but characterized that program as one primarily for the sick and aged without comment about the increased use of public aid by the unemployed; see Boston Finance Commission, *Reports,* 1922–23, 1923–24.

31. Overseers of the Poor, *Annual Report,* 1920; Overseers of Public Welfare, *Annual Report,* 1929. Adjusted for the cost of living, Mothers' Aid expenditures increased 27 percent. Research by the Children's Bureau noted a national trend toward decreased funding of Mothers' Aid programs in the 1920s. On this, see Emma Octavia Lundberg, "Progress of Mothers' Aid Administration," *Social Service Review* 2 (September 1928): 435–8.

Historian Joanne Goodwin found Chicago to be an exception to this trend and credits the expansion of the mothers' pension program there in the 1920s to the network of female reformers associated with Hull House; see *Gender and the Politics*, 145–55.

Chapter 4. Private Charities, 1920–1929

1. Scholars of American welfare history tend to mute the different responses of private charity organizations to the enlargement of public welfare in the 1920s. Generalizing, they argue that private organizations moved away from relief and toward social services during the 1920s, foreshadowing the surrender of most relief activities to public welfare in the 1930s. The retreat from relief, they argue, represented a philosophical as well as a practical convergence among private charities, related to the emergence of the social work profession. The more optimistic among these scholars claim that social workers improved the operations of private charities by introducing professional standards of care for the poor. More critical scholars insist that the development of social services, as well as the social work profession in general, reflected the enduring power of white middle-class Protestants to determine cultural norms and, thereby, to ensure their continued control over the poor and less powerful. By and large, historians of women likewise advance a critical interpretation of social services, putting most of the blame for its cultural domination on the Anglo-Saxon women who dominated the early social work field. Examples of the more optimistic interpretation are: Roy Lubove, *The Struggle for Social Security, 1900–1935*, 2d ed. (Pittsburgh: University of Pittsburgh Press, 1989, orig. 1968); Walter I. Trattner, *From Poor Law to Welfare State: A History of Social Welfare in America*, 6th ed. (New York: Free Press, 1999); Michael B. Katz, *In the Shadow of the Poorhouse* (New York: Basic Books, 2000); and James T. Patterson, *America's Struggle against Poverty* (Cambridge: Harvard University Press, 1994). An example of the more critical interpretation is Brian Gratton, "Social Workers and Old Age Pensions," *Social Service Review* 57 (September 1983): 403–15. An early study of women's influence on private charity work is Anthony Platt, *The Child Savers: The Invention of Delinquency*, 2d ed. (Chicago: University of Chicago Press, 1977). Later studies include Molly Ladd-Taylor, *Mother-Work: Women, Child Welfare, and the State, 1890–1930* (Chicago: University of Illinois Press, 1994), and Linda Gordon, *Pitied but Not Entitled: Single Mothers and the History of Welfare* (New York: Free Press, 1994). More than Ladd-Taylor, Gordon recognizes diverse voices among female social workers; her conclusion, nevertheless, is that Anglo-Saxon ideas about charity dominated the formation of the American welfare system. Matthew A. Crenson's history of the development of foster care highlights the influence of Catholic and Jewish charities on public welfare policy. In *Building the Invisible Orphanage: A Prehistory of the American Welfare State*, Crenson explores the differences between private charities and argues that diversity of religious charities contributed to the fragmented nature of the American welfare system (Cambridge: Harvard

University Press, 1998). Scholars of Catholic history have also insisted on the influence of religion on social welfare but have offered little comparison between Catholic charities and other private organizations. See Kenneth J. Heineman, *A Catholic New Deal: Religion and Reform in Depression Pittsburgh* (University Park: Pennsylvania State Press, 1999); Dorothy M. Brown and Elizabeth McKeown, *The Poor Belong to Us: Catholic Charities and American Welfare* (Cambridge: Harvard University Press, 1997).

2. In her study of programs for unmarried mothers, historian Regina G. Kunzel also notes the limited influence of professional social work on the practices of charities and homes for unwed mothers in the 1920s; see Regina G. Kunzel, *Fallen Women, Problem Girls: Unmarried Mothers and the Professionalization of Social Work, 1890–1945* (New Haven: Yale University Press, 1993), 3.

3. The Overseers traditionally provided $1 or $2 a week to poor families. In contrast, Mothers' Aid grants ranged from $6 to $12.

4. BPA, *Annual Report,* 1920–23, 6–7, *Annual Report,* 1926–27, 11.

5. Examples of the argument against an old age pension are: Richard K. Conant, "Proposed Measures for Improving the Care of the Aged in Massachusetts," *Proceedings of the National Conference of Social Work* (New York: Columbia University Press, 1926): 562–4; Francis Bardwell, "Public Outdoor Relief and the Care of the Aged in Massachusetts," *Social Service Review* 4 (June 1930): 199–209; and Boston Council of Social Agencies (CSA) *Bulletin* 5 (January 1926): 8. On the outcome of the campaign, see Gratton, "Social Workers and Old Age Pensions."

6. Family Welfare Society (FWS), "The Faith That Is in Us," *Annual Report,* 1922.

7. FWS, *Annual Report,* 1922.

8. The Finance Commission was a governor-appointed board that acted as a "watchdog" over municipal administration and spending. During the 1920s, Yankee Republicans dominated its membership. On the Finance Commission, see Constance Burns, "Irony of Progressive Reform: Boston, 1898–1910," in *Boston 1700–1980: The Evolution of Urban Politics,* ed. Ronald P. Formisano and Constance K. Burns (Westport, Conn.: Greenwood Press, 1984), 113–64.

9. William H. Pear, "The Joint Operations of Family Helping Agencies in Boston," *The Family* (October 1925), 159–67.

10. In fact, public aid never fully supported the families it aided, but the Mothers' Aid program did provide a larger weekly benefit than any private charity or the Overseers had.

11. The FWS increased its annual expenditures on salaries from $15,936 in 1920 to $95,663 in 1928 while maintaining a staff of approximately sixty. The BPA's annual expenditures on salaries increased from $14,714 in 1920 to $20,205 in 1928 while its staff remained at eight. Figures on salaries are from Commonwealth of Massachusetts, Board of Charity (Board of Public Welfare, after 1922), *Annual Report,* 1920, 1928; FWS, *Annual Report,* 1922.

12. In its earliest days, the 1870s and 1880s, the Associated Charities had, in fact, refused to dispense any poor relief. On the early history of the Associated Charities, see

Nathan I. Huggins, *Protestants against Poverty: Boston's Charities, 1870–1900* (Westport, Conn.: Greenwood, 1971); FWS, *Annual Report,* 1920, 8–9.

13. Before 1913, widows had made up a third of the BPA's relief cases, but within two years of the Mothers' Aid bill, widows represented only 14 percent of its cases. In contrast, unemployed families had grown from 28 percent of its cases in 1912–13 to nearly half of its cases during the twenties. The FWS did not give comparative figures, but its annual reports in the late twenties suggest that work with families with unemployed men was replacing work with widows and women with children. The 1928 report linked 56 percent of the families aided to unemployment; only 27 percent were attributed to desertion, nonsupport, and other marital difficulties.

14. On psychiatric social work, see Clarke A. Chambers, "Creative Effort in an Age of Normalcy, 1918–33," *Social Welfare Forum* (New York: Columbia University Press, 1961); and Trattner, *From Poor Law,* 260–3. Psychiatric social work did not gain widespread popularity or application until after World War II, but it did influence the Protestant charity network in the Northeast as early as the 1920s; see Kunzel, *Fallen Women, Problem Girls,* 146–7; FWS, *Annual Report,* 1922.

15. Family Welfare Society, "Family Problems in Immigrant Groups," by Dr. George LaPiana, *Annual Report,* 1924, 3–16. LaPiana was a professor at Harvard and president of the FWS's North End Conference, meaning he oversaw the work of the staff and volunteer visitors working in the North End, an Italian neighborhood near Boston harbor. His name suggests that he was not Protestant, but the conclusions of his study reflected the general attitudes of the FWS.

16. FWS, *Annual Report,* 1920.

17. In its 1920 *Annual Report,* the FWS mentioned its support of legislation "to provide the equal rights of women in blanket terms," suggesting that it supported efforts for an Equal Rights Amendment; aside from this comment, however, the FWS took no clear position on women's rights. Likewise, the BPA's reports mentioned neither the woman's suffrage campaign nor the struggle over the ERA.

18. FWS, "Women and Children in Industry," by Charles Boyden, *Annual Report,* 1926–27, 5–22. Three female social workers did the "actual work of compilation" of the report; however, the male leadership of the FWS supported the report's conclusion. Introducing it, the president of the FWS, John F. Moors, wrote: "Imagine how difficult it must be for a woman to be of good courage who has worked all day away from home and yet must prepare the breakfast and support for her family and otherwise be a good mother to her children."

19. For information on the activities of the Catholic Charitable Bureau, this chapter relies on typewritten annual reports written by the directors and submitted to the archbishop of the Boston Archdiocese. In his study of the Catholic Charitable Bureau, Daniel McLellan identified Elizabeth Moloney, the state supervisor of Mothers' Aid, as a Catholic although he did not find any specific ties between Moloney and the CCB; see Daniel McLellan, "A History of the Catholic Charitable Bureau of the Archdiocese of Boston"

(Ph.D. diss., University of Notre Dame, 1984), 86; CCB, Annual Report, 1922, Catholic Charitable Bureau Files, Archives of the Archdiocese of Boston.

20. CCB, Annual Report, 1920; Gratton, "Social Workers and Old Age Pensions," 407.

21. CCB, Annual Report, 1924; controversy over the expense of the renovation delayed the opening until March 1926, by which time Nichols was mayor.

22. On the political activities of the Boston Archdiocese, see James M. O'Toole, *Militant and Triumphant: William Henry O'Connell and the Catholic Church in Boston, 1859–1944* (Notre Dame, Ind.: University of Notre Dame, 1992), 121–42, and "Prelates and Politicos: Catholics and Politics in Massachusetts, 1900–1970," in *Catholic Boston: Studies in Religion and Community, 1870–1970* (Boston: Roman Catholic Archbishop of Boston, 1985), 15–65, and Brown and McKeown, *The Poor Belong to Us*, 57–8.

23. CCB, Annual Report, 1920. Referenda in 1915 and 1916 suggested strong popular support for public old age pensions, especially in Boston. See Theda Skocpol, *Protecting Soldiers and Mothers: The Political Origins of Social Policy in the United States* (Cambridge: Harvard University Press, 1992), 269, and Christopher Anglim and Brian Gratton, "Organized Labor and Old Age Pensions," *International Journal of Aging and Human Development* 25 (1987): 99–101.

24. CCB, Annual Report, 1922. Paula Kane astutely discusses the cultural resistance embedded within Catholic assimilation; see *Separatism and Subculture: Boston Catholicism, 1900–1920* (Chapel Hill: University of North Carolina Press, 1994).

25. For information on the CCB expansion into outlying cities, such as Lawrence and Lowell, see McLellan, "A History," chap. 3. The Bureau's first neighborhood house was the North End Guild, opened in 1922. The following year a second neighborhood center was opened in the West End, followed by others in the South End, South Boston, Roxbury, and Charlestown. Daniel McLellan contends that these neighborhood centers differed from Protestant-led settlement houses in that they focused on specific services related to children and did not engage in larger social reform activities; see McLellan, "A History," chap. 4. The Bureau's relief expenditures increased yearly during the 1920s. According to its 1926 annual report, the Bureau disbursed $49,951 in relief that year, compared with $14,000 in 1922, a 256-percent increase. Even adjusted for inflation, this represented a 238-percent increase.

26. Susan Walton, "To Preserve the Faith: Catholic Charities in Boston, 1870–1930," in *Catholic Boston: Studies in Religion and Community, 1870–1970*, ed. Robert E. Sullivan and James M. O'Toole (Boston: Roman Catholic Archbishop of Boston, 1985), 67–119.

27. McLellan, "A History," 86. The Boston College School of Social Work opened in 1936. The CCB's director commented that it was "an effort to develop students trained in modern techniques and methods of social work and at the same time have that training vitalized and interpreted by a philosophy which was truly Catholic"; see CCB, Annual Report, 1936. Brown and McKeown discuss the influence of the professional social work theories on Catholic charity leaders, but they stress the uncertainty and even resistance to professional training for Catholic charity workers; see *The Poor Belong to Us*, 73–85. Kane

also notes the suspicion among Catholic leaders toward professional social work education, particularly for women; see *Separatism and Subculture,* 247.

28. CCB, Annual Report, 1926. Kane's work on Boston Catholicism includes an extended discussion of the gender roles prescribed by the Church, and she argues that its antimodernism, in fact, helped mediate the emergence of a Catholic middle class; see *Separatism and Subculture,* 320–2.

29. Hecht was appointed to the Board of Overseers in 1908 and served as its chairman between 1920 and 1926. Silverman served as the joint superintendent of the Federated and the United Hebrew Benevolent Association from 1912 to 1917. She had been the assistant to her predecessor, Max Mitchell. Upon his retirement, she was hired as temporary superintendent but then remained in the position for five years. In her study of Jewish charity in Boston, historian Barbara Solomon contends that Silverman's appointment "surprised those who had resisted the idea of a woman executive." On Silverman, see *Pioneers in Service: The History of the Associated Jewish Philanthropies of Boston* (Boston: Associated Jewish Philanthropies, 1956), 77; Federated Jewish Charities (FJC), *Report of the Welfare Committee,* 5, in the Papers of the Combined Jewish Philanthropies (PCJP), box 3, folder 2, American Jewish Historical Society.

30. Gratton, "Social Workers and Old Age Pensions," 406.

31. According to one source, the Overseers complained of being "'crowded' by the UHBA in connection with Mothers' Aid"; see Ferdinand Berl, "History of the Jewish Community of Boston," 54–5, box 1, folder 4, PCJP. Jacob J. Kaplan, a Federated representative, participated in a study group to set a standard budget for public welfare cases when a ruling on Mothers' Aid cases counted private charity as income; see Solomon, *Pioneers,* 106–7.

32. General District Service, Annual Report, 1924–25, box 3, folder 5, PCJP. In 1921, the District Service program distributed $36,517 in relief; it distributed $48,829 in 1925; "Auditors Reports, 1920–32," box 4, folder 1, PCJP.

33. District Centers were opened in Roxbury, Dorchester, East Boston, the West End, and the South End. See Solomon, *Pioneers,* 106–13. One often-cited example of Catholic women's restricted activities is the exchange between Archbishop William Henry O'Connell and CCB director Father Michael J. Scanlan in which both criticized the League of Catholic Women for cooperating with non-Catholic welfare organizations; see Walton, "To Preserve," 112–3. The Federated lodged no similar criticism against its female social workers who were actively involved in nonsectarian organizations and professional associations.

34. In 1924–25, the District Centers aided 2,357 families; 1,199 of these cases involved families with father, mother, and children in the home. Other groups aided included married couples without children (103), widows with dependent children (339), widowers with dependent children (115), deserted families (89), divorced or separated families (167), single residents (80), transients (217), and unclassified (48). Figures are from General District Service, Annual Report, 1924–25, box 3, folder 5, PCJP.

35. Council of Social Agencies, *Bulletin,* January 1927.

36. Subscriptions, the word used then for number of donors, fell from 6,002 in 1920 to 3,645 in 1929; see Berl, "History of the Jewish Community of Boston," 108. On suburban migration of Boston's Jews in the 1920s, see Gerald H. Gamm, *Urban Exodus: Why the Jews Left Boston and the Catholics Stayed* (Cambridge: Harvard University Press, 1999), 184–216.

37. For example, see Dora Margolis, "Strengthening Jewish Family Life," *Combined Jewish Appeal, Year Book—1945,* 83–6, box 2, PCJP.

38. Other organizations included the League for Preventive Work, the Men's Monday Lunch Club, the Women's Monday Lunch Club, and the Boston Federation of Settlements.

39. In 1922, the officers included James Jackson, president; Joseph J. Tillinghast, vice president; James J. Phelan, treasurer; and Gertrude W. Peabody, clerk. Ten of the eleven members of the executive committee were also Yankee Protestants, the exception being Rev. Michael J. Scanlan of the Catholic Charitable Bureau; see CSA, *Bulletin,* February 1922, 3.

40. On charges of racial segregation, see CSA, *Bulletin* (December 1931), 5–6. One study of the CSA in Cincinnati found that the organization took an active role in the civil rights movement in that city during the 1940s and 1950s. The CSA did not play a similar role in Boston at the same time. With its smaller black population, Boston did not confront its racial divisions until post–World War II migration increased the city's black population. On Cincinnati, see Andrea T. Kornbluh, "'The Bowl of Promise': The Cincinnati Council of Social Agencies" (Ph.D. diss., University of Cincinnati, 1983).

41. CCB, Annual Report, 1922; on the Community Chest effort in Boston, see Janis H. Moravec, "A History of Joint Financing Among Social and Health Agencies of Boston, Massachusetts" (master's thesis, Simmons College, 1948).

Chapter 5. The Thirties

1. Studies of the social welfare policies of the 1930s usually focus on the policies and initiatives of the New Deal. Only a few have considered the policies of that period in a broader time frame than the crisis of the Depression. Even state and municipal studies of the 1930s, including the historian Charles H. Trout's *Boston, the Great Depression, and the New Deal* (New York: Oxford University Press, 1977), primarily evaluate the impact of federal programs on local politics. Picking up the story in 1929, these studies miss the connections between earlier welfare policies and the developments in the 1930s. Linda Gordon's work on single mothers and the history of welfare is a notable example of a study with a broader chronological framework. Gordon traces welfare policy related to single mothers from the late nineteenth century through the creation of the federal Aid to Dependent Children (ADC) program in 1935. See *Pitied but Not Entitled: Single Mothers and the History of Welfare* (New York: Free Press, 1994). Studies on the effect of the New Deal on specific localities include *The New Deal: The State and Local Levels,* ed. John Braeman, Robert H. Bremner, David Brody (Columbus: Ohio State University

Press, 1975). This volume includes an article by Harold Gorvine, "The New Deal in Massachusetts," that provided helpful background information, 3–43; more detailed investigations of the impact of the New Deal on urban centers include Trout, *Boston;* Jo Ann E. Argersinger, *Toward a New Deal in Baltimore* (Chapel Hill: University of North Carolina Press, 1988); Lizabeth Cohen, *Making a New Deal: Industrial Workers in Chicago, 1919–1939* (New York: Cambridge University Press, 1990); Leonard Leader, *Los Angeles and the Great Depression* (New York: Garland, 1991); and John F. Bauman, "The City, the Depression, and Relief: The Philadelphia Experience, 1929–1939" (Ph.D. diss., Rutgers University, 1969). Cohen begins her study of Chicago in 1919, which gives her book a broader frame. For an overview of literature on urban sites and the New Deal, see Charles H. Trout, "The New Deal and the Cities," in *Fifty Years Later: The New Deal Evaluated,* ed. Harvard Sitkoff (Philadelphia: Temple University Press, 1985), 133–53. In an innovative recent study of the relief and work programs of the 1930s, the sociologist Edwin Amenta links New Deal work relief and unemployment policy to its implementation in various states. He argues that the lack of democratic politics in the South limited the scope of the national programs and eventually curtailed federal social programs. See *Bold Relief: Institutional Politics and the Origins of Modern American Social Policy* (Princeton: Princeton University Press, 1998).

2. Ann Orloff and Theda Skocpol have cited Civil War pensions as an earlier example of federal social provision. However, since the military pensions were not means tested, I do not consider them as either the equivalent or predecessors of later public assistance programs that were federally funded. For their argument, see Ann Shola Orloff, "The Political Origins of America's Belated Welfare State," in *The Politics of Social Policy in the United States,* ed. Margaret Weir, Ann Shola Orloff, and Theda Skocpol (Princeton: Princeton University Press, 1988), 37–80, especially 45–52, and Theda Skocpol, *Protecting Soldiers and Mothers: The Political Origins of Social Policy in the United States* (Cambridge: Harvard University Press, 1992), 102–51.

3. On Boston's economic strengths and liabilities going into the Depression, see Trout, *Boston,* 3–26. The joblessness rate in Boston was slightly lower than in New York and Chicago, but higher than that in Cleveland and Detroit; see Trout, *Boston,* 81. Between 1929 and 1933, wages dropped 54.2 percent in Boston, only slightly less than the 56.7 percent drop in other areas; Trout, *Boston, 76,* 81.

4. Trout, *Boston,* 81.

5. Public relief expenditures have been figured using data from the *Annual Reports* of Boston's public welfare department, which was the Overseers of the Poor (OP) until 1922, when it was renamed the Overseers of the Public Welfare (OPW). These reports were published separately and as part of the *Documents of the City of Boston, 1926–1941.* According to a survey of 120 cities, the average per capita expenditure in 1931 was $1.20 on public relief and $0.36 on private relief; in Boston the averages were $5.74 and $0.49. That same year the overall average monthly public relief grant was $21.34 whereas the average monthly grant in Boston was $45.16. U.S. Department of Labor, Children's Bureau,

Trends in Different Types of Public and Private Relief in Urban Areas, 1929–35, by Emma A. Winslow, no. 237 (Washington, D.C., 1937).

6. Boston *Globe,* November 26, 1935; *PCCB,* May 15, 1933; Martha Gellhorn to Hopkins, quoted in Trout, *Boston,* 174.

7. OPW, *Annual Report,* 1928, 1933; *PCCB,* March 19, 1934.

8. Information on the unemployed comes from three studies: Alice Channing, "A Study of Unemployed Clients of Boston Family and Relief Agencies," *Bulletin,* Council of Social Agencies, Boston (December 1931), 11–18; Mary A. Clapp, "Further Studies of Unemployed Clients of Boston Social Agencies," *Bulletin,* Council of Social Agencies, Boston (June 1932), 2–14; Eleanor S. Washburn, "More About Unemployed Clients of the Boston Department of Public Welfare," *Bulletin,* Council of Social Agencies, Boston (June–July 1933), 1–8.

9. Suzanne Mettler explores the way unemployment programs, though potentially open to both men and women, tended to aid only men; see *Dividing Citizens: Gender and Federalism in New Deal Public Policy* (Ithaca: Cornell University Press, 1998).

10. The Overseers of the Public Welfare saw their caseload among the native-born increase from 37.9 percent in 1929, to 50.8 percent in 1931, to 61.8 percent in 1932. The Associated Jewish Philanthropies showed a far higher percentage of foreign-born clients both before and during the thirties, but the Protestant relief agencies and the public welfare department saw an increase in the number of native-born clients during the 1930s; see Clapp, "Further Studies," 5.

11. The 1928 caseload was 6,777; see OPW, *Annual Report,* 1928, 1932. The cost of living decreased during this period, making the increase slightly larger in real terms; see OP, *Annual Report,* 1929, 1933. In 1929, poor relief expenditures made up 6.4 percent of the city budget; see Trout, *Boston,* 285, 86.

12. On voluntarism of the Hoover years and its influence on Boston, see Trout, *Boston,* chap. 5; on the opposition to public unemployment relief, see Janis H. Moravec, "A History of Joint Financing among Social and Health Agencies of Boston," master's thesis, Simmons College, 1948. Private relief in Boston, excluding the Catholic Charitable Bureau, amounted to $333,064 ($0.43 per capita) in 1929; it totaled $2,452,597 ($3.14 per capita) in 1932. Although comparable data on the CCB's relief expenditures is not available, what information is available indicates that its inclusion would drive the percentage increase higher. The CCB's relief disbursements increased 124 percent between 1931 and 1932, from $122,811 to $275,357; see CCB, Annual Report, 1932, CCB files, Archives of the Archdiocese of Boston. On the comparison of increase in public and private relief between 1929 and 1932, public relief increased 306 percent (from $2,751,829 to $11,194,076); private relief, excluding Catholic charities, increased 636 percent (from $333,063 to $2,452,597); see Winslow, *Trends,* 76.

13. In their studies of the CCB, both Daniel McLellan and Susan Walton have noted the increased focus on religious mission among the CCB leadership during the 1930s. See Daniel McLellan, "A History of the Catholic Charitable Bureau of the Archdiocese of

Boston" (Ph.D. diss., University of Notre Dame, 1984), chap. 5, and Susan Walton, "To Preserve the Faith: Catholic Charities in Boston, 1870–1930," in *Catholic Boston: Studies in Religion and Community, 1870–1930,* ed. Robert E. Sullivan and James M. O'Toole (Boston: Roman Catholic Archbishop of Boston, 1985), 67–119. The CCB did not record the specific number of families it aided, but said 146,307 families visited its district offices in 1932; see CCB, Annual Report, 1932.

14. In 1933, the FWA aided 2,060 relief cases; see Ferdinand Berl, "History of the Jewish Community of Boston," 215, PCJP, box 1, folder 4, American Jewish Historical Society. The average monthly relief was $20.87, high compared with allocations of other private agencies and of the public welfare department; see Winslow, *Trends,* 118; Dora Margolis, "Strengthening Jewish Family Life," *Combined Jewish Appeal, Yearbook—1945,* 83–6, PCJP, box 2.

15. The expenditures of the FWS rose from $265,965 in 1930 to $405,186 in 1934; the BPA increased its expenditures from $75,702 to $157,040 during the same period. Figures from: Commonwealth of Massachusetts, Department of Public Welfare (DPW), *Annual Report,* 1930, 1934. Weekly grants from the BPA and FWS were approximately $4.50; see Winslow, *Trends,* 115.

16. Papers of the United Community Services of Metropolitan Boston, unprocessed, Boston Public Library.

17. On the conservatism of the church and the CCB's criticism of the New Deal, see Daniel McLellan, "A History of the Catholic Charitable Bureau of the Archdiocese of Boston" (Ph.D. diss., University of Notre Dame, 1984), 187; Trout, *Boston,* 259–63.

18. On Jewish support for Roosevelt, see Gerald Gamm, *The Making of New Deal Democrats: Voting Behavior and Realignment in Boston, 1920–1940* (Chicago: University of Chicago Press, 1989), chap. 2. For examples of Jewish support for the New Deal, see Boston *Globe,* October 2, 1935, and October 21, 1935. Trout also discusses the AJP's support of New Deal programs; see *Boston,* 267–8.

19. During the 1920s, there had been significant discussion in the leading social work periodicals concerning public welfare reform and professionalization. Examples include S. P. Breckingridge, "Frontiers of Control in Public Welfare," *Social Service Review* 1 (March 1927): 84–99, and Albert G. Ritchie, "The State's Responsibility for Social Welfare," *Social Forces* 4 (March 1926): 608–10. Leaders of Boston's social work community, including leaders of the Protestant charities, participated in this discussion. See Robert W. Kelso, "State Board Progress," *Proceedings of the National Conference of Social Work* (New York: Columbia University Press, 1917), 338–9; Richard K. Conant, "Difficulties in the Administration of Public Welfare Departments and Their Responsibilities," *Proceedings of the National Conference of Social Work* (1924): 551–4. On the change in attitude among Protestant charity leaders, see BPA, *Annual Report,* 1927 to 1938 (published as one report in 1939). Quotation from Eva Whiting White, "Public Welfare Explained," *North, East, West, South* 2, no. 1 (1933), Papers of Eva Whiting White, box 1, folder 5, The Arthur and Elizabeth Schlesinger Library, Radcliffe Institute for Advanced Study at Harvard University. White was part of the Protestant social work network in Boston. She

served on the Overseers of the Public Welfare and was a leader in the settlement move-ment in Boston. On appointments of Protestant charity leaders to New Deal agencies, see Trout, *Boston*, 164–5.

20. Expenditures by private charities were $2,452,597 in 1932; they were $1,335,791 in 1933. By 1935, they had fallen to $886,930; see Winslow, *Trends*, 78.

21. Inaugural speech before the City Council, *PCCB*, January 1, 1934.

22. *PCCB*, September 26, 1932.

23. On the campaign against public welfare, see Barry J. Kaplan, "Reformers and Charity: The Abolition of Public Relief in New York City, 1870–1898," *Social Service Review* 52 (1978): 202–14; on criticisms of Civil War pensions, see Theda Skocpol, *Protecting Soldiers and Mothers*, chap. 2.

24. *PCCB*, March 19, 1934, and May 7, 1934.

25. *PCCB*, August 4, 1930.

26. The Finance Commission, the chief investigative agency of the city, was no longer controlled by Yankee Republicans. In 1930, as a favor to Mayor Curley, Governor Frank G. Allen had appointed Frank A. Goodwin to the Finance Commission. According to Curley biographer Jack Beatty, Goodwin proved "an accommodating commission chair-man"; see *The Rascal King: The Life and Times of James Michael Curley (1874–1958)* (Read-ing, Mass.: Addison-Wesley, 1992), 347. On investigation by police, see *PCCB*, January 14, 1932, and Boston *Globe*, August 12–31, 1932.

27. The investigations recommended replacing the Board of Overseers with a single paid commissioner of public welfare appointed by the mayor. With Curley in City Hall, the Republican-dominated state legislature, along with Henry Lee Shattuck on the City Council and the representatives of the city's Protestant-led charities, opposed this re-form. On the effort to reform the Overseers of the Public Welfare, see Papers of Henry Lee Shattuck, box 48, folder 5, Massachusetts Historical Society, and Council of Social Agen-cies, *Bulletin*, June–July 1934.

28. *PCCB*, March 19, 1934; January 5, 1933; May 7, 1934.

29. Criticisms of welfare recipients included antagonistic remarks about aliens re-ceiving aid. As one councilman put it: "We go on voting thousands and thousands of dol-lars for the Tomasellos, the Singarellas and the Sarsaparillas . . . and have nothing for the poor fellows who really need to be taken care of." *PCCB*, September 26, 1932. See also: February 2, 1927; March 20, 1933; March 19, 1935; July 12 and 26, 1937; August 9, 1937; August 20, 1937.

30. *City Record*, July 19 and 26, 1930, 815–6.

31. Commonwealth of Massachusetts, DPW, *Annual Report*, 1930, 2.

32. For men, the projects included working at milk distribution centers and com-modities warehouses, completing subway extensions, and rebuilding beaches. For women, there were sewing projects, work in canneries, and housekeeping assignments. In the mid-thirties approximately 24 percent of the city's unemployed received Works Progress Administration (WPA) funds; see Trout, *Boston*, 183–4. On restrictions of the

programs to "breadwinners," see Robert Washburn to Harry Hopkins, March 2, 1934, Papers of Harry Hopkins, box 59, Franklin D. Roosevelt Library. Nancy E. Rose's history of work relief during the 1930s, *Put to Work: Relief Programs of the Great Depression* (New York: Monthly Review Press, 1994), also outlines the federal work programs' sexual discrimination. Historian Alice Kessler-Harris examines the gender and racial limitation of the New Deal programs in her article, "In the Nation's Image: The Gendered Limits of Social Citizenship in the Depression Era," *Journal of American History* 86, no. 3 (December 1999): 1251–79. On ethnic and racial discrimination in the work programs in Boston and response by black organizations, see Trout, *Boston,* 191–2; for an excellent discussion of the role of black women in the emerging political voice of African Americans in Boston, see Sarah Deutsch, *Women and the City: Gender, Space, and Power in Boston, 1870–1940* (New York: Oxford University Press, 2000), 264–79.

33. On Boston's, and specifically Curley's, relationship with President Roosevelt and the New Deal agencies, see Trout, *Boston,* chap. 7.

34. *PCCB,* June 10, 1935; July 15, 1935; July 26, 1935; August 30, 1937.

35. *PCCB,* March 23, 1935; November 12, 1935; May 6, 1935. Henry Lee Shattuck founded the Municipal Research Bureau (MRB) in 1930 as a private, nonprofit organization that would evaluate the financial workings of the city. The MRB did a number of studies of welfare expenditures during the 1930s and advocated that the city attempt to qualify for whatever federal funds were available in order to keep its own budget down; see *PCCB,* October 7, 1935. Trout, *Boston,* 310.

36. OPW, *Annual Report,* 1929, 1939. The increase is in spending not adjusted for cost of living since there was little change during the decade. Boston's population decreased 4 percent in the 1930s, dropping from 805,000 in 1929 to 770,816 in 1940. On adjustments to the municipal budget, see Trout, *Boston,* 286.

37. Finance Commission, *Report to the Mayor Relative to the Investigation of the Department of Public Welfare,* July 3, 1931; *PCCB,* May 1, 1933. The percentage of Dependent Aid cases that were identified as caused by unemployment were: 1929: 26 percent; 1930: 41 percent; 1931: 69 percent; 1932: 75 percent; 1933: 76 percent; 1934: 74 percent; see OPW, *Annual Report,* 1929–34. The transfer of the elderly clients to Old Age Assistance (OAA) also affected these percentages.

38. On the effect of federal funds on local programs, see Martha Derthick, *The Influence of Federal Grants: Public Assistance in Massachusetts* (Cambridge: Harvard University Press, 1970).

39. For a history of the campaign for OAA in Massachusetts, see Alton A. Linford, *Old Age Assistance in Massachusetts* (Chicago: University of Chicago Press, 1949). For more recent analyses of the state's Old Age program, see Brian Gratton, *Urban Elders: Family, Work, and Welfare among Boston's Aged, 1890–1950* (Philadelphia: Temple University Press, 1986). Ann Shola Orloff and Theda Skocpol both cite the prolonged and ultimately unsuccessful campaign in Massachusetts for an old age pension as an example of the political constraints to the formation of an American welfare state during the Progressive

era; see Orloff, *The Politics of Pensions: A Comparative Analysis of Britain, Canada, and the United States, 1880–1940* (Madison: University of Wisconsin Press, 1993), and Skocpol, *Protecting Soldiers and Mothers, 267–85*. On labor support, see Christopher Anglim and Brian Gratton, "Organized Labor and Old Age Pensions," *International Journal of Aging and Human Development* 25 (1987): 91–107.

40. On the debates on aid to the elderly, see Richard K. Conant, "Proposed Measures for Improving the Care of the Aged in Massachusetts," *Proceedings of the Conference of Social Work* (1926): 562–64, and Lucille Eaves, *Aged Clients of Boston's Social Agencies* (Boston: Women's Educational and Industrial Union, 1925). On the opposition to old age pensions, see Brian Gratton, "Social Workers and Old Age Pension," *Social Service Review* (September 1983), 403–15, and Skocpol, *Protecting Soldiers and Mothers, 267–72*.

41. Commonwealth of Massachusetts, DPW, *Annual Report*, 1931, 17.

42. In his study of OAA in Boston, Brian Gratton relates the increased demands on the program to the growing proportion of the elderly in the city. See *Urban Elders*, chap. 2; on Protestant charities' response to the growth of OAA, see *Urban Elders*, 170; Commonwealth of Massachusetts, DPW, *Annual Report*, 1932, 1935.

43. *PCCB*, October 26, 1936; January 11, February 8, May 3, 1937.

44. Commonwealth of Massachusetts, DPW, *Annual Report*, 1932, 1931.

45. The elderly made up 33 percent of Dependent Aid cases in 1929; this had dropped to 15 percent by 1933 and to 3 percent by 1937. OPW, *Annual Report*, 1929, 1933, 1937; Gratton, *Urban Elders*, 162–6; Commonwealth of Massachusetts, DPW, *Annual Report*, 1936.

46. Linda Gordon found the same phenomenon on the national level in her study of single mothers and welfare policy; see *Pitied but Not Entitled*, 251.

47. Mothers' Aid cases increased 70 percent, from 975 to 1,658, between 1929 and 1934; see OPW, *Annual Report*, 1929, 1934; Commonwealth of Massachusetts, DPW, *Annual Report*, 1931.

48. In a national study of Mothers' Aid programs, the Children's Bureau reported that the average monthly grant per family in Boston dropped from $73.03 in 1931 to $70.80 in 1932; see U.S. Department of Labor, Children's Bureau, *Mothers' Aid, 1931*, no. 220 (Washington, 1933), 36; OPW, *Annual Report*, 1921, 1931; Commonwealth of Massachusetts, DPW, *Annual Report*, 1930–38.

49. Commonwealth of Massachusetts, DPW, *Annual Report*, 1932.

50. OPW, *Annual Report*, 1930–39; Commonwealth of Massachusetts, DPW, *Annual Report*, 1932.

51. Expenditures on ADC in Boston were $1,430,865 in 1937, and they increased to $2,572,004 in 1939; see OPW, *Annual Report*, 1937, 1939. On the development of the ADC program and its focus on children, see Linda Gordon, "Putting Children First: Women, Maternalism, and Welfare in the Early Twentieth Century" in *U.S. History as Women's History: New Feminist Essays*, ed. Linda K. Kerber, Alice Kessler-Harris, and Kathryn Kish Sklar (Chapel Hill: University of North Carolina Press, 1995), 63–86. Gordon argues that a focus on children did not guarantee adequate funding or political support.

52. Between 1929 and 1939, direct relief to the poor increased from $2,480,382 to $12,840,894; see OPW, *Annual Report*, 1929, 1939.

53. MRB, *Bulletin*, no. 70, August 5, 1938, 3.

54. On the 1939 amendments, see Alice Kessler-Harris, "Designing Women and Old Fools: The Construction of the Social Security Amendments of 1939," in *U.S. History as Women's History*, 94–100; *In Pursuit of Equality: Women, Men, and the Quest for Economic Citizenship in 20th-Century America* (New York: Oxford University Press, 2001), 135–6.

55. On the welfare reforms of the late thirties, see Commonwealth of Massachusetts, DPW, *Annual Report*, 1939; William Haber, "The Public Welfare Problem in Massachusetts," *Social Service Review*, June 1938: 179–204; and William Haber and Herman M. Somers, "The Administration of Public Assistance in Massachusetts," *Social Service Review*, September 1938: 397–569.

56. R. Clyde White, *Public Welfare Administrative Survey, City of Boston* (Boston: Finance Commission, 1948).

Conclusion. Placing Boston in Social Policy Theories

1. Louis Hartz, *The Liberal Tradition in America* (New York: Harcourt, Brace & World, 1955), is the most commonly cited example of the liberal interpretation. Overviews of postwar welfare policy include: James T. Patterson, *America's Struggle against Poverty in the Twentieth Century* (Cambridge: Harvard University Press, 2000); Walter I. Trattner, *From Poor Law to Welfare State: A History of Social Welfare in America* (New York: Free Press, 1999); and Charles Nobel, *Welfare as We Knew It: A Political History of the American Welfare State* (New York: Oxford University Press, 1997).

2. Gosta Esping-Andersen, *The Three Worlds of Welfare Capitalism* (Princeton: Princeton University Press, 1990), is perhaps the best example of comparative study of welfare regimes that casts the United States as a liberal state.

3. Margaret Weir, Ann Shola Orloff, and Theda Skocpol's introduction to their edited volume, *The Politics of Social Policy in the United States*, is a good example of the effort to consider American political institutions and their relation to the development of welfare policy (Princeton: Princeton University Press, 1988). Theda Skocpol contrasts "maternal" and "paternal" welfare programs in *Protecting Soldiers and Mothers: The Political Origins of Social Policy in the United States* (Cambridge: Harvard University Press, 1992). Edwin Amenta, in *Bold Relief: Institutional Politics and the Origins of Modern American Social Policy* (Princeton: Princeton University Press, 1998), focuses on constraints posed by the failure of democracy in the South. Suzanne Mettler, in *Dividing Citizens: Gender and Federalism in New Deal Public Policy* (Ithaca: Cornell University Press, 1998), argues that implementation of welfare policy resulted in inequities in social provision.

4. On race, gender, and welfare policy, see Eileen Boris, "The Racialized Gendered State: Construction of Citizenship in the United States," *Social Politics* 2 (summer 1995): 160–80; Gwendolyn Mink, *The Wages of Motherhood: Inequality in the Welfare State*,

1917–1942 (Ithaca: Cornell University Press, 1995); Jill Quadagno, *The Color of Welfare* (New York: Oxford University Press, 1994), and Linda Gordon, *Pitied but Not Entitled: Single Mothers and the History of Welfare* (New York: Free Press, 1994).

5. Alice Kessler-Harris, "In the Nation's Image: The Gendered Limits of Social Citizenship in the Depression Era," *Journal of American History* 86, no. 3 (December 1999): 1251–79.

6. Here I contrast the works by James Connelly and Sarah Deutsch, *The Triumph of Ethnic Progressivism: Urban Political Culture in Boston, 1900–1925* (Cambridge: Harvard University Press, 1998) and *Women and the City: Gender, Space, and Power in Boston, 1870–1940* (New York: Oxford University Press, 2000).

7. For a selection of Marshall's work, see *Class, Citizenship, and Social Development: Essays by T. H. Marshall,* ed. Seymour Martin Lipset (Westport, Conn.: Greenwood Press, 1973). Michael Katz explores Marshall's applicability to the U.S. welfare system in his book *The Price of Citizenship: Redefining the American Welfare State* (New York: Metropolitan Books, 2001), 343–7.

8. Alice Kessler-Harris argues that "economic citizenship," defined as "the achievement of an independent and relatively autonomous status that marks self-respect and provides access to the full play of power and influence that defines participation in a democratic society," was simultaneously enhanced and restricted by the welfare policy in the United States. See *In Pursuit of Equity: Women, Men, and the Quest for Economic Citizenship in 20th-Century America* (New York: Oxford University Press, 2001), quotation from 14. A critique of Marshall by Nancy Fraser and Linda Gordon has informed my thinking here; see "Civil Citizenship against Social Citizenship?" in *The Condition of Citizenship,* ed. Bart van Steenbertgen (London: Sage Publications, 1994).

INDEX

adequate support, 27, 36, 41, 48, 51, 67, 70, 111, 114

African Americans, 9, 10, 11, 88, 92, 94, 104–5, 121, 127 n.6, 128 n.8, 150 n.40

aid in kind, 13, 17

Aid to Dependent Children (ADC), 5, 108, 110–2, 113–6, 156 n.51. *See also* Mothers' Aid

Amenta, Edwin, 150 n.1

Americanization, 78

Archdiocese of Boston. *See* Catholic Archdiocese

Associated Charities (AC), 14, 15–8, 40, 73, 77, 146 n.12. *See also* Family Welfare Society (FWS); Protestant charities

Associated Jewish Philanthropies (AJP), 86–7, 98. *See also* Federated Jewish Charities (FJC); Jewish charities

Baker, Paula, 136 n.31

Bardwell, Francis, 109

blacks. *See* African Americans

boss, 10, 54, 64

Boston, 8–12; charitable institutions, 10–1; charity system, 13–5, 31, 39, 121; compared with other cities, 11; and Depression, 91–5; political setting, 9–10, 54, 120–1; social context, 8–9, 54; social mobility in, 9

Boston College, 82, 148 n.27

Boston Provident Association (BPA), 14, 15–8, 40, 73–9, 87, 97, 146 n.11, 147 n.13, 153 n.15. *See also* Protestant charities

Brackett, Jeffrey R., 78, 87

Brandeis, Louis, 33

breadwinner, 3, 4, 12, 29, 30, 49, 53, 59, 60, 77, 89, 93, 96, 104, 119, 120, 122

cases. *See* recipients

case studies, 46–8, 76, 86, 99

caseworkers. *See* social workers

casework methodology, 3, 17, 68, 72, 76, 85, 87, 88. *See also* social work

categorical aid programs, 5, 90, 106, 108–12

Catholic Archdiocese (Boston), 18–9, 20, 81–2, 98

Catholic Charitable Bureau, 18–21, 33, 38, 50, 79–84, 88–9, 96, 152 n.13. *See also* Catholic charities

Catholic charities, 70–9, 121–2; and Council of Social Agencies, 75, 88–9; on dependency, 80, 82–3, 96; on family relations, 20, 82–3; leaders of, 18, 20, 38, 80, 88; and Mothers' Aid, 50–1, 79–80; and New Deal, 98; on old age pensions, 33, 38, 81; on poverty, 19, 35; and public welfare, 19, 73, 79–80, 98; on social work, 20–1, 82; on unemployment, 22, 96; and widows' pension campaign, 33, 35, 38, 131 n.13; on women, 3–4, 20, 22, 50–1, 79, 82–3, 149 n.33. *See also* private charities

Catholicism, 83, 98, 149 n.28

Catholics, 15, 19–20, 45, 81, 82, 96, 98; influence, 6, 80; Irish, 9, 127 n.8

charities. *See* private charities

Charity Building, 13–4, 80, 95, 99. *See also* Hawkins Street; public welfare: building

Children's Aid Society, 40

Children's Bureau, 46, 47

child welfare, 19, 21, 26, 34–5, 38, 81

City Charter, 54–5, 67, 140 n.5, 142 n.17

City Council, 26, 56–9, 106; and Mothers' Aid, 63–4; and New Deal, 106; and Old Age Assistance, 110; and Overseers, 60–1, 63, 100, 101, 102–4; and poverty, 59, 101; and private charities, 59; and social work, 62, 63; and unemployment, 59–60; and welfare recipients, 61–4, 101–4; and work relief, 105

Civil War pensions, 101, 118, 151 n.2

Susan Traverso earned her Ph.D. in American history at the University of Wisconsin-Madison. She is associate professor of history at North Central College, where she teaches American social and political history and in the college's History of Ideas and Gender and Women's Studies programs. She lives in Naperville, Illinois, with her husband and two children.